Greenhouse Gas Reduction Through State and Local Transportation Planning

The DOT Center for Climate Change & Environmental Forecasting

Final Report September 2003

U.S. Department of Transportation

I0437748

Notice

This document is disseminated under the sponsorship of the Department of Transportation in the interest of information exchange. The United States Government assumes no liability for its contents or use thereof.

REPORT DOCUMENTATION PAGE

Form Approved
OMB No. 0704-0188

Public reporting burden for this collection of information is estimated to average 1 hour per response, including the time for reviewing instructions, searching existing data sources, gathering and maintaining the data needed, and completing and reviewing the collection of information. Send comments regarding this burden estimate or any other aspect of this collection of information, including suggestions for reducing this burden, to Washington Headquarters Services, Directorate for Information Operations and Reports, 1215 Jefferson Davis Highway, Suite 1204, Arlington, VA 22202-4302, and to the Office of Management and Budget, Paperwork Reduction Project (0704-0188), Washington, DC 20503.

1. AGENCY USE ONLY (Leave blank)	2. REPORT DATE September 2003	3. REPORT TYPE AND DATES COVERED Final Report October 2001-August 2003

4. TITLE AND SUBTITLE	5. FUNDING NUMBERS
Greenhouse Gas Reduction Through State and Local Transportation Planning	RS391/P3073

6. AUTHOR(S)
William M. Lyons, Scott Peterson, Kimberly Noerager

7. PERFORMING ORGANIZATION NAME(S) AND ADDRESS(ES)	8. PERFORMING ORGANIZATION REPORT NUMBER
U.S. Department of Transportation John A. Volpe National Transportation Systems Center 55 Broadway Cambridge, MA 02142	DOT-VNTSC-RSPA-03-02

9. SPONSORING/MONITORING AGENCY NAME(S) AND ADDRESS(ES)	10. SPONSORING/MONITORING AGENCY REPORT NUMBER
U.S. Department of Transportation Research and Special Programs Administration 400 7th Street, S.W. Washington, D.C. 20590	

11. SUPPLEMENTARY NOTES

12a. DISTRIBUTION/AVAILABILITY STATEMENT	12b. DISTRIBUTION CODE
This document is available to the public through the National Technical Information Service, Springfield, Virginia 22161.	

13. ABSTRACT (Maximum 200 words)

This report will improve understanding of how states and localities might contribute to greenhouse gas (GHG) emissions reduction through transportation planning. Transportation is a major contributor to GHG emissions. State and local transportation planning affects transportation decisions, which, in turn, can influence travel patterns, land use, energy consumption, and, ultimately, GHG emissions.

The amount of activity by states and local areas to develop GHG and climate change plans is impressive. States and local areas undertake these activities voluntarily. Typically, these areas make commitments to conduct a baseline GHG emissions analysis, set local GHG reduction targets, develop local action plans, implement emissions reduction policies, and monitor progress.

This report uses seven case studies to evaluate how states and local areas are using transportation planning to pursue goals to reduce GHG emissions. The research focuses on the broad transportation planning process, strategies and other actions selected, and GHG emission reductions accomplished or projected. This report considers both transportation planning by state Departments of Transportation, metropolitan planning organizations, city and county transportation agencies, and transportation operators, and energy, environmental, or land use planning by other state and local agencies that considers climate change and transportation policies, investments, and strategies.

14. SUBJECT TERMS	15. NUMBER OF PAGES
greenhouse gas, climate change action plan, GHG Plans, CO_2 Plans, transportation planning	92
	16. PRICE CODE

17. SECURITY CLASSIFICATION OF REPORT Unclassified	18. SECURITY CLASSIFICATION OF THIS PAGE Unclassified	19. SECURITY CLASSIFICATION OF ABSTRACT Unclassified	20. LIMITATION OF ABSTRACT Unlimited

NSN 7540-01-280-5500

Standard Form 298 (Rev. 2-89)
Prescribed by ANSI Std. 239-18
298-102

METRIC/ENGLISH CONVERSION FACTORS

ENGLISH TO METRIC | METRIC TO ENGLISH

LENGTH (APPROXIMATE)

ENGLISH TO METRIC	METRIC TO ENGLISH
1 inch (in) = 2.5 centimeters (cm)	1 millimeter (mm) = 0.04 inch (in)
1 foot (ft) = 30 centimeters (cm)	1 centimeter (cm) = 0.4 inch (in)
1 yard (yd) = 0.9 meter (m)	1 meter (m) = 3.3 feet (ft)
1 mile (mi) = 1.6 kilometers (km)	1 meter (m) = 1.1 yards (yd)
	1 kilometer (km) = 0.6 mile (mi)

AREA (APPROXIMATE)

ENGLISH TO METRIC	METRIC TO ENGLISH
1 square inch (sq in, in^2) = 6.5 square centimeters (cm^2)	1 square centimeter (cm^2) = 0.16 square inch (sq in, in^2)
1 square foot (sq ft, ft^2) = 0.09 square meter (m^2)	1 square meter (m^2) = 1.2 square yards (sq yd, yd^2)
1 square yard (sq yd, yd^2) = 0.8 square meter (m^2)	1 square kilometer (km^2) = 0.4 square mile (sq mi, mi^2)
1 square mile (sq mi, mi^2) = 2.6 square kilometers (km^2)	10,000 square meters (m^2) = 1 hectare (ha) = 2.5 acres
1 acre = 0.4 hectare (he) = 4,000 square meters (m^2)	

MASS - WEIGHT (APPROXIMATE)

ENGLISH TO METRIC	METRIC TO ENGLISH
1 ounce (oz) = 28 grams (gm)	1 gram (gm) = 0.036 ounce (oz)
1 pound (lb) = 0.45 kilogram (kg)	1 kilogram (kg) = 2.2 pounds (lb)
1 short ton = 2,000 pounds (lb) = 0.9 tonne (t)	1 tonne (t) = 1,000 kilograms (kg) = 1.1 short tons

VOLUME (APPROXIMATE)

ENGLISH TO METRIC	METRIC TO ENGLISH
1 teaspoon (tsp) = 5 milliliters (ml)	1 milliliter (ml) = 0.03 fluid ounce (fl oz)
1 tablespoon (tbsp) = 15 milliliters (ml)	1 liter (l) = 2.1 pints (pt)
1 fluid ounce (fl oz) = 30 milliliters (ml)	1 liter (l) = 1.06 quarts (qt)
1 cup (c) = 0.24 liter (l)	1 liter (l) = 0.26 gallon (gal)
1 pint (pt) = 0.47 liter (l)	
1 quart (qt) = 0.96 liter (l)	
1 gallon (gal) = 3.8 liters (l)	
1 cubic foot (cu ft, ft^3) = 0.03 cubic meter (m^3)	1 cubic meter (m^3) = 36 cubic feet (cu ft, ft^3)
1 cubic yard (cu yd, yd^3) = 0.76 cubic meter (m^3)	1 cubic meter (m^3) = 1.3 cubic yards (cu yd, yd^3)

TEMPERATURE (EXACT)

ENGLISH TO METRIC	METRIC TO ENGLISH
$[(x-32)(5/9)]$ °F = y °C	$[(9/5) y + 32]$ °C = x °F

QUICK INCH - CENTIMETER LENGTH CONVERSION

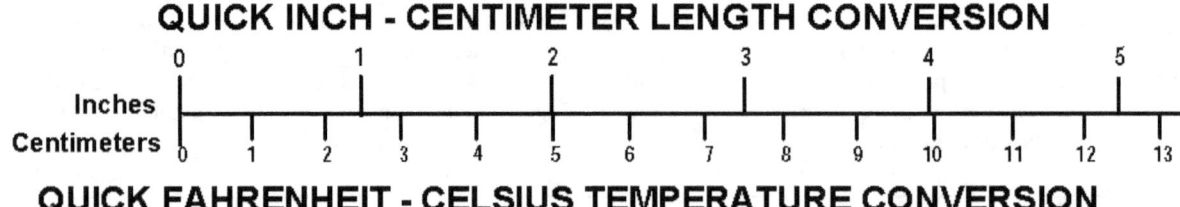

QUICK FAHRENHEIT - CELSIUS TEMPERATURE CONVERSION

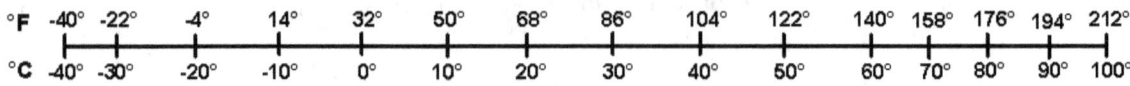

For more exact and or other conversion factors, see NIST Miscellaneous Publication 286, Units of Weights and Measures.
Price $2.50 SD Catalog No. C13 10286

Updated 6/17/98

Acknowledgments

This report was prepared for the U.S. Department of Transportation's (USDOT) Center for Climate Change and Environmental Forecasting (CCCEF) by the USDOT Volpe National Transportation Systems Center (Volpe Center). The report presents the results of a study on how states and local areas use the transportation planning process to pursue goals to reduce greenhouse gas (GHG) emissions.

The project team consisted of William M. Lyons, project manager, Scott Peterson, and Kim Noerager. Sara McKinstry and Kate Klotz assisted with editing. Diane Turchetta of the Federal Highway Administration coordinated the project for the CCCEF. The project team received helpful assistance and advice, including suggestions on candidate areas for case studies and information about state and local planning processes, from the following groups and contacts:

- U.S. Environmental Protection Agency (EPA), State and Local Partners Program: Steve Dunn, Denise Mulholland, and Andrea Denny of the State and Local Capacity Building Branch.
- International Council for Local Environmental Initiatives: Nancy Skinner, International Director; Abby Young, U.S. Director of Cities for Climate Protection; and Melissa Royael, Senior Technical Assistance Associate.
- International City/County Management Association: Jennifer Folta, Assistant Project Manager for Environmental Programs.
- Delaware: John Byrne, Director, and Leigh Glover, Center for Energy and Environmental Policy at the University of Delaware.
- King County, Washington: Ann Martin, Principal Transportation Planner.
- Madison, Wisconsin: David Benzschawel, Environmental Manager.
- New England Governors' Conference, Inc.: John Shea, Director of Energy and Environment Programs.
- New Jersey: Michael Winka, Administrator, Office of Innovative Technology and Market Development, and Athena Sarafides, New Jersey Department of Environmental Protection.
- Portland, Oregon: Susan Anderson, Director, and Michael Armstrong, Policy Analyst, Office of Sustainable Development.
- Seattle, Washington: David Allen and Jemae Hoffman, Seattle Department of Transportation Mobility Management Group, and Kim Drury, Environmental Program Manager, Office of Sustainability and Environment.

The research team also gained insights from the session on integrated transportation, energy, and climate change planning at the EPA's Fifth State and Local Climate Change Partners' Conference, co-sponsored by the USDOT's CCCEF, in November 2002 (http://www.epa.gov/global warming/annapolis). Local contacts were given the opportunity to review and comment on drafts of this report. However, please note that local contacts and the CCCEF are not responsible for the accuracy of the report, which is solely the responsibility of the research team.

This report is available on the USDOT's CCCEF web site at http://www.dot.gov/climate. A hard copy can be obtained by e-mail (lyons@volpe.dot.gov) or by fax ((617) 494-3260).

Table of Contents

Table of Contents (cont.)

List of Figures

List of Tables

Executive Summary

Transportation is a major contributor to greenhouse gas (GHG) emissions. State and local transportation planning directly affects transportation decisions, which in turn can influence travel patterns, land use, energy consumption, and, ultimately, GHG emissions. This research will improve understanding of how states and localities might contribute to GHG emissions reduction through transportation planning. The research will also assist the U.S. Department of Transportation (USDOT) by identifying opportunities to integrate global climate change considerations and GHG emissions reductions into programs and policies.

The amount of activity by states and local areas to develop GHG and climate change plans is impressive. States and local areas are undertaking these activities voluntarily, in the absence of federal requirements. Twenty-five states, plus Puerto Rico, have initiated GHG plans; 19 have completed plans; and 37 have initiated or completed GHG inventories. In addition, 134 cities and counties are participating in an initiative to reduce local GHG emissions. These local participants have made commitments to conduct a baseline GHG emissions analysis, set local GHG reduction targets, develop a local action plan, implement emissions reduction policies, and monitor progress.

This report uses seven case studies to evaluate how states and local areas are using transportation planning to pursue goals to reduce GHG emissions. Information is current as of the time of the research from 2001 to early 2003.

This research was not intended to critically examine the assumptions, methods, data, or likely success of the initiatives in the state and local area plans discussed in the case studies. Such a critical examination was beyond the scope of this limited study. The actions identified in the plans, which typically include projections of reductions in GHG emissions, are presented in this report as they are in their respective plans. In the future, states, local areas, and other interested parties may find it extremely valuable for the USDOT Center for Climate Change and Environmental Forecasting (CCCEF) or another independent entity to undertake such an objective assessment.

The research focuses on the broad transportation planning process, strategies and other actions selected, and GHG emission reductions accomplished or projected. This report considers both:

- Traditional transportation planning undertaken by all state DOTs, metropolitan planning organizations, city and county transportation agencies, and transportation operators, and
- Energy, environmental, or land use planning by other state and local agencies that considers climate change and transportation policies, investments, and strategies.

Based on analysis of planning processes in the case study areas, this report offers the following observations:

- **A coordinated formal approach is important.** The planning elements used in the case study areas provide a framework for interested states and local areas to adapt to their unique situations. These elements include: description of regional impacts; assessment of GHG emissions baselines; emissions reduction goals; and an action plan to reduce emissions. This framework provides a useful alternative to taking an ad hoc approach to beginning a new GHG plan.

- **Climate change impacts can be used as points of departure.** Recognition of the regional impacts states or local areas face from climate change can be a critical impetus for developing GHG plans. Impacts reflect the unique vulnerabilities of each area – shorelines in New Jersey, Oregon, and Washington, for example, or forests and tourism in New Hampshire.

- **Motivation to act does not come solely from concern over impacts.** Local areas may conduct GHG planning out of a sense of local responsibility and a need to contribute to actions underway by other areas, but areas may also participate in GHG planning out of a pragmatic understanding that climate change goals can strengthen other state and local initiatives. For example, Madison, Wisconsin, Delaware, and New Jersey's GHG planning is closely linked to city or state energy policy.

- **Smart growth and energy conservation planning can provide the foundation for climate change planning.** Climate change planning does not appear to originate independently. Rather, most case study areas are built on the planning foundations already established for related concerns, including energy (i.e., conservation and development of alternative sources and industries) and smart growth (i.e., balancing land use and economic development considerations). For example, Seattle's GHG planning is closely linked to smart growth, energy conservation, and air quality.

- **Political champions play a critical role.** Political champions play a critical role in initiating and supporting GHG plans. Leadership from the Mayors and elected Commissioners or Councilors was critical to the success of GHG planning in Madison, Wisconsin, and Portland, Oregon. The GHG initiative of the New England Governors and Eastern Canadian Premiers (NEG-ECP) is led by the bipartisan governors and premiers.

- **Non-transportation agencies are playing lead roles.** Much of the impetus for state and local GHG plans appears to come from state and local agencies with primary responsibility for non-transportation sectors such as energy, environment, and land use. The University of Delaware plays a key role as convener for Delaware's GHG planning, the city environmental manager coordinates GHG planning in Madison, and the Department of Environmental Protection is the lead in New Jersey's GHG planning.

- **The transportation sector appears to lag behind in GHG emissions reduction planning.** Although the transportation sector is consistently identified as a major source of GHG emissions, transportation policies, strategies, and actions to reduce emissions typically lag behind those for other sectors. Recommended transportation actions tend to be more conceptual, framed as general policy, and less specific in terms of timetables and institutional responsibilities for implementation.

- **A range of institutional approaches and integration methods exists.** No single best approach exists for defining institutional roles and responsibilities to successfully integrate climate change and transportation planning. The case study areas include the NEG-ECP, a multistate/bi-national initiative, complementary city and county initiatives in Seattle, and state initiatives in Delaware and New Jersey.

- **Success depends on a broad base of support and long-term commitment.** The case study areas demonstrate that moving from the ideals of a GHG plan to the actual implementation of plan actions is difficult and requires a long-term time horizon and the cooperation of different levels of government, different economic sectors, and public and private partners. GHG planning in Portland began formally with adaptation of the GHG Plan in 1993, and has continued through later planning, implementation, and evaluation stages. Delaware demonstrated continuity with its broad base of institutional and personal commitment to a long-term planning process.

- **Incremental progress is valuable.** Several case study areas recognized the value of demonstrating early incremental progress, beginning with strategies where benefits clearly surpass financial and political costs and where lead agencies have direct responsibility. Portland and New Jersey demonstrate that actions that can be quantified and quickly accomplished establish credibility for future initiatives.

- **It is difficult to tell if the glass is "half empty" or "half full."** The case study areas uniformly recognize the significant contribution that the transportation sector makes to baseline GHG emissions and the important role that it might play in GHG emissions reduction. However, explicit GHG reduction linkages to transportation planning are at an early stage, newly formed, and rapidly evolving. For example, New Jersey will have a future focus on transportation after initial successes with industries, utilities, and education sectors.

- **Continued evolution will be necessary to move from indirect supportive actions to explicit planning.** The case study areas are already pursuing strategies for smart growth/livability, congestion, and air quality improvements that also reduce GHG emissions. Opportunities exist to further develop climate change plans by building on these supportive initiatives through explicit consideration of how these strategies can also save energy, and reduce GHG emissions, while meeting traditional transportation goals. The cities of Portland and Madison have direct operational responsibilities for major transportation programs, making it easier to implement transportation actions in their GHG plans. Seattle transportation agencies are implementing aggressive programs to reduce automobile use through expanded transit, ridesharing, telecommuting, and improved pedestrian and bicycle facilities.

- **Peer experiences can demonstrate successful GHG planning.** States and local areas are very interested in descriptions and documentation of successful GHG planning by peers. Such peer exchanges may be the best way to demonstrate that climate change goals and planning can be introduced in a rational manner without threatening the goals and programs of transportation agencies. According to one state program manager, it would be invaluable for Commissioners who have initiated GHG planning to share experiences with Commissioners considering beginning a similar process.

- **Additional research would prove valuable.** While this study provides a perspective on how several states and local areas are beginning to integrate GHG emission reduction goals into transportation planning, it would be worthwhile to conduct additional research in the future. It would be valuable for an independent entity to assess these efforts in the future, including tracking lessons learned and actual GHG emission reductions.

I. INTRODUCTION

The U.S. Department of Transportation's (USDOT) Volpe National Transportation Systems Center (Volpe Center) completed this report for the USDOT Center for Climate Change and Environmental Forecasting (CCCEF). The CCCEF is dedicated to fostering awareness of the potential links between transportation and global climate change and formulating related policy solutions.

Research Questions

- *Incentives* – Why are agencies combining global climate change goals with mobility, economic development, and other traditional transportation goals?
- *Methodologies* – What indicators, forecast models, and other techniques are applied?
- *Win-Win Opportunities* – How can global climate change goals complement state and local transportation goals, including improving accessibility, reducing congestion and energy use, and encouraging smart growth?
- *Institutional Structures* – What institutional structures support transportation decisions that reduce GHG emissions?
- *Public and Political Support* – How was public and political support gained?
- *Results* – What are the completed or projected reductions in carbon equivalents?

Transportation is a major contributor to greenhouse gas (GHG) emissions. State and local transportation planning has major impacts on transportation decisions, which in turn influence travel patterns, land use, energy consumption, and, ultimately, GHG emissions.

This research evaluates how states, metropolitan planning organizations (MPOs), cities, and transportation providers are using transportation planning to pursue goals to reduce GHG emissions. Focusing on the broad transportation planning process, strategies and other actions selected, and GHG emission reductions accomplished or projected, the research first considers traditional transportation planning undertaken by all state DOTs, MPOs, and city and county transportation agencies. The research then considers the climate change and transportation policies, investments, and strategies that are part of the energy, environmental, and land use planning efforts of state and local agencies.

The goal of this report is to improve understanding of how states and localities might contribute to GHG reduction. This research uses seven case studies to discuss how states and localities can reduce GHG emissions through transportation planning.[1] The overall intent is to generate ideas other states and localities can use to connect transportation and GHG planning and to balance climate change goals with the traditional transportation goals of mobility, accessibility, and congestion relief. In addition, this research will assist the USDOT in identifying opportunities to integrate climate change and GHG reduction goals into USDOT programs and policies and to encourage further linkages.

This research was not intended to critically examine the assumptions, methods, data, or likely success of the initiatives in the state and local area plans discussed in the case studies. Such a critical examination was beyond the scope of this limited study. The actions identified in the

---

[1] Since information is current as of the time of the research in 2001 to early 2003, and activities in the case study areas are rapidly evolving, readers are encouraged to review web sites of the case study areas for updated information.

plans, which typically include projections of reductions in GHG emissions, are presented in this report as they are in their respective plans. In the future, states, local areas, and other interested parties may find it valuable for an independent entity such as the USDOT CCCEF to undertake such an objective assessment.

States and localities consistently identify transportation as a major source of GHG emissions. In baseline GHG inventories for state, regions, and cities, transportation typically accounts for 30 percent or more of total GHG emissions. Since state and local transportation planning can have impacts on travel patterns, land use decisions, and energy consumption, this planning is also likely to impact GHG emissions. As a result, states and localities may be able to use the transportation planning process to reduce their GHG emissions and climate change "footprint."

An impressive number of states and localities are developing GHG emissions reduction plans.[2] Appendix B lists the cities and counties participating in the International Council for Local Environmental Initiatives' (ICLEI) Cities for Climate Protection Campaign (CCPC). Even more impressive, these states and localities are undertaking these activities voluntarily, in the absence of federal requirements. As part of these activities, participating areas are conducting baseline GHG emissions analyses, setting local GHG reduction targets, developing local action plans, implementing emissions reduction policies, and monitoring progress to reduce GHG.[3]

> **Who Has GHG Plans?**
>
> - 25 states and Puerto Rico are initiating plans.
> - 19 states have completed plans.
> - 37 states have initiated or completed GHG inventories.
> - 134 cities and counties are participating in a national initiative to reduce local GHG emissions.

However, while many states and localities include transportation strategies and policies in their action plans to reduce GHG, most rely to a great extent on non-transportation strategies. A 2002 Volpe Center study for the Federal Highway Administration found that none of the 48 state DOT long-range transportation plans reviewed included substantive reference to climate change goals, despite frequent references to environmental, smart growth, and "livability" goals and policies and strong support of GHG plans by many governors.[4] Many state transportation plans may lack climate change components as they predate more recent state and local GHG planning efforts. In many cases, linkages between transportation and GHG planning are newly formed and rapidly evolving.

---

[2] Numbers are according to the ICLEI and the EPA, which encourages these efforts through the State and Local Partners Program. The program provides technical advice, training, and financial assistance (http://yosemite.epa.gov/globalwarming/ghg.nsf/actions/StateActionPlans?Open).
[3] Source: http://www.iclei.org/us/ccp/milestoneprocess html.
[4] Source: http://www.fhwa.dot.gov/hep10/state/evalplans htm.

1. SELECTION OF CASE STUDIES

This report presents case studies on four local areas, two states, and one bi-national region. Case studies were chosen based on the following criteria:

Case Studies
• New England Governors and Eastern Canadian Premiers (NEG-ECP)
• New Jersey
• Delaware
• Portland, Oregon
• Seattle and King County, Washington
• Madison, Wisconsin

- Recommendations by peer agencies and associations involved in climate change programs.
- Willingness of local participants to provide information.
- Availability of technical and other documentation.
- Implementation of innovations that could be used as nationwide examples.

2. METHODOLOGY AND APPROACH TO THE TRANSPORTATION PLANNING PROCESS

This analysis uses a transportation planning process framework derived from the Intermodal Surface Transportation Efficiency Act (ISTEA), which covered 1992-1997, and its reauthorization act, the Transportation Equity Act for the 21st Century (TEA-21). ISTEA and TEA-21 define a comprehensive, continuous, and cooperative transportation planning process that each state and metropolitan area adjusts to reflect its unique circumstances, goals, and long-range priorities.

Under TEA-21, the major products of the statewide and metropolitan transportation planning processes are a 20-year strategic long-range plan and a 3- to 5-year program of investments. Key characteristics of the statewide and metropolitan-area planning processes, as described in TEA-21, include:

- A strategic look at how best to balance locally defined long-range traditional transportation concerns (e.g., congestion relief, mobility, or accessibility) with broader concerns (e.g., economic development, reduced air pollution, or GHG emissions).
- Broad participation of public citizens, advocacy groups, the private sector, and organizations that are not traditional participants in transportation planning but that have an interest in and impact on transportation (e.g., environmental, energy, and land use agencies).
- Financially realistic planning achieved by matching projected costs to revenues in the short and long terms.
- Consideration of a broad range of socioeconomic factors.
- Linkages to other planning processes with close connections to transportation, such as air quality and land use planning.

Transportation planning typically focuses on the activities of state DOTs, federally designated MPOs, city and county transportation agencies, and public transit, port, rail, and airport authorities and other transportation operators. This report takes a broader focus on transportation planning. Since climate change is a new and evolving concern for state and local transportation agencies, this research also analyzes selected state and local energy and environmental plans with transportation and climate change focuses. Of particular interest is the ability of state and local agencies to connect this energy and environmental planning to the planning and decision-making processes led by state DOTs, MPOs, city transportation agencies, and transportation providers.

State and local area GHG plans are often linked to energy planning and conservation or air quality planning. These efforts are typically initiated by state or local energy or environmental agencies and consider transportation in terms of goals, analysis of trends, and investments and strategies to reduce GHG emissions. (Appendix A provides a map of states with these GHG planning initiatives.) Of the state and local GHG plans reviewed for this report, all include transportation as a GHG emissions contributor and transportation policies and strategies as items in their action plans.

Figure 1 provides a simplified framework for a broad approach to transportation planning that considers GHG reductions. Well-established links between transportation planning processes and GHG, smart growth, or sustainable development planning are indicated with solid lines, and evolving links are indicated with broken lines. The traditional transportation planning process is identified with shaded boxes. This framework indicates how the planning processes of non-transportation agencies, such as state energy or environmental agencies, can be linked to the traditional planning processes of state DOTs and MPOs. In many cases, states and localities begin to connect traditional and non-traditional transportation planning as they conduct GHG, smart growth, or sustainable development planning. Linking these planning processes can help states and localities identify and implement GHG reductions. The research team used this framework to study and compare the processes observed in the case study areas.

4

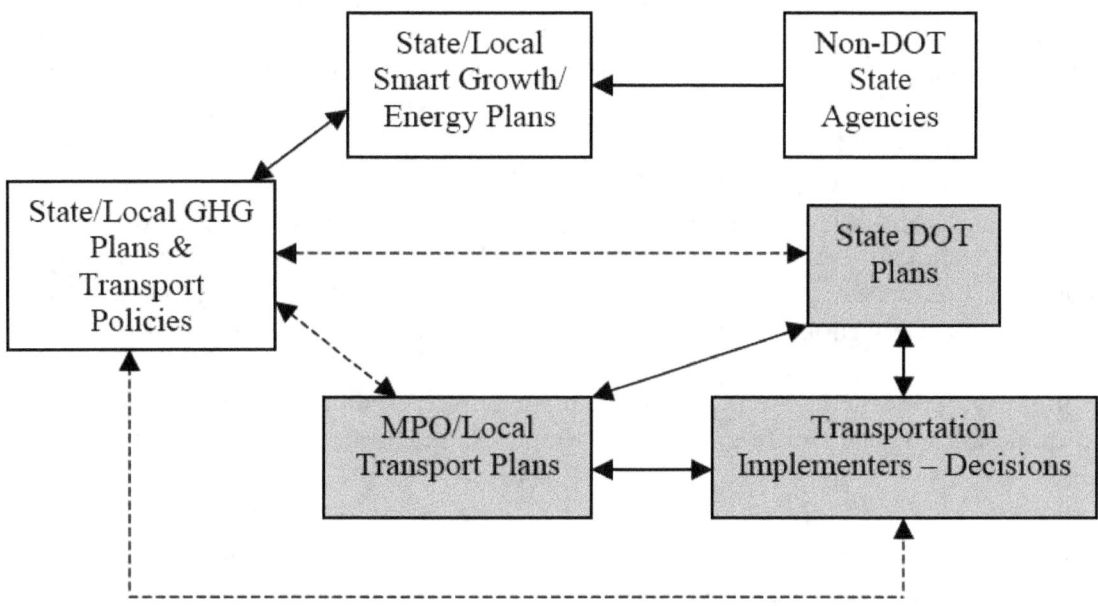

Figure 1. Framework for Transportation Planning Process

The research team looked for early indications of a path toward integration of transportation and climate change planning and evolving linkages. Such planning integration and linkages involve more than placing a GHG reduction goal alongside typical mobility, accessibility, or congestion relief goals or federally required air quality improvement goals in a long-range plan for an air quality non-attainment area and more than using a criterion for GHG reduction (e.g., tons of carbon equivalent) as one among other factors to select alternative transportation projects. Instead, a connection, however modest, might be demonstrated by consideration of climate change:

- And regional impacts for transportation in a public information forum set up as part of the development of a transportation plan;
- Within the policy statement in the 20-year metropolitan plan;
- In a 50-year vision plan developed by many regions; or
- Through participation of state DOT planners on a technical advisory committee for the state energy agency's GHG plan.

The research team focused on the broadly defined transportation and GHG planning processes and did not review the GHG emission reductions local participants identified or forecast nor the methodologies they applied. Rather than considering the GHG emission reductions of specific transportation projects, strategies, or policies, this report considers how the transportation planning process can be used to support these decisions. The research team reviewed individual state and local processes to identify insights that might be of interest to a wider audience.

This report makes a subtle but critical distinction between assigning GHG emission reductions to decisions that have already been made and using an ongoing planning process that incorporates GHG reduction goals into future decision-making. Assigning GHG reductions retroactively to decisions is useful for climate change planning because it establishes a technical process for measuring the GHG impacts of transportation and raises public and decision-maker awareness of the connections between transportation and GHG. While the connections between transportation and GHG can be helpful for future planning, this "after-the-fact" connection is not the focus of this research. Instead, this research examines the development of planning processes that incorporate GHG reduction as a substantive goal alongside other traditional transportation goals, such as congestion relief, mobility, access to employment, and improved air quality.

The research team used the following guide to evaluate how each case study is using transportation planning to identify policies, investments, and strategies to reduce GHG emissions.

- Is there a strategy or action plan directed toward reducing GHG emissions?
- At what level is the planning?
  - Multistate
  - Statewide
  - Regional
  - Local
- Who is the lead agency?
- What other agencies participate?
- What type of plan or planning process is used?
  - Transportation plan
  - GHG emissions reduction plan
  - Energy plan
  - Environmental plan
  - Comprehensive/land use plan (e.g., "smart growth," "livable communities," "sustainability")
- Is there a distinct and significant transportation element?
- Is a GHG baseline defined with inventory?
- Are anticipated GHG reductions clearly identified?
- Is there a reasonable basis to anticipate that these results can be achieved?
  - Is a finite time period set for achieving results?
  - Are there qualitative measures to define success?
  - Are there quantitative measures to define success?
- Are there explicit linkages between climate change and transportation planning processes?
  - How are transportation planning agencies and their planning processes involved? (Specify state DOT, city DOT, MPOs, regional agencies, port, or airport.)
  - What is the involvement of agencies representing other sectors? (Specify energy,

environment, health and human services, economic development/commerce, physical planning, emergency response, etc.)

- – What is the involvement of different levels of government? (Specify federal, state, regional, or local governments.)
- Are action plans or other credible means provided to implement strategies or recommendations? Or do plans appear to be endpoints?
- Are roles and responsibilities for implementation or other next steps identified?
- How are transportation-implementing agencies involved? (Specify state DOT, city DOT, transit operators, port, airport, private sector (e.g., freight), etc.)

The research team focused on the broad outlines of complex state and local planning processes. The analysis relied on technical reports and other documentation, and, when possible, conducted telephone interviews with a limited number of local officials who play lead roles in GHG planning and who could take a broad view of the process.

II. CASE STUDIES

1. NEW ENGLAND GOVERNORS AND EASTERN CANADIAN PREMIERS (NEG-ECP)

1.1 Introduction

The New England Governors and Eastern Canadian Premiers (NEG-ECP) addressed climate change and GHG emissions issues at its conference in July 2000. The conference established the political and policy foundation for regional climate change initiatives, including an action plan to complement other regional, state, local, and provincial initiatives. NEG-ECP is composed of the states of Vermont, Rhode Island, New Hampshire, Massachusetts, Connecticut, and Maine, and the provinces of New Brunswick, Newfoundland and Labrador, Nova Scotia, Prince Edward Island, and Quebec.

NEG-ECP's work is based on a number of scientific and policy concerns. For example, the New England Regional Assessment, "Preparing for a Changing Climate: The Potential Consequences of Climate Variability and Change," which was conducted for the U.S. Global Change Research Program, concluded that New England and upstate New York have warmed 0.7 degrees Fahrenheit in the last 100 years. Researchers predict that temperatures will continue to rise 6 to 10 degrees by the end of this century. According to the report, the potential impacts from climate change on New England and Eastern Canada include the following:

- Deterioration of air quality.
- Significantly increased health risks.
- Altered ecosystems.
- Economic impacts to the health sector, tourism, and the natural resource industry.

1.2 Approach

NEG-ECP recognizes that global climate change may have serious impacts on the New England-Eastern Canadian region. The NEG-ECP believes it is prudent to undertake multistate/ multiprovince preventative and adaptive measures to mitigate the impacts of climate change. In July 2000, NEG-ECP adopted Resolution 25-9, which recognizes that climate change could have a serious impact on the region's environment and economy. Upon adoption of this resolution, NEG-ECP directed its Committee on the Environment, the Northeast International Committee on Energy (NICE), and the New Brunswick Premier's National Round Table on the Environment and the Economy (NRTEE) to work together to develop a strategic plan consistent with the Canadian National Implementation Strategy for Climate Change. The result is the Climate Change Action Plan, the culmination of efforts between the NEG, the ECP, and their respective energy and environmental agencies.

1.2.1 Who Is Involved and Why

In 1937, the governors of Vermont, Rhode Island, New Hampshire, Massachusetts, Connecticut, and Maine formally established the New England Governors' Conference (NEGC) as a voluntary alliance of states to promote New England's economic development. The region's six governors serve on NEGC's board of directors and implement policies and programs designed to respond to regional issues. NEGC coordinates regional policy programs in economic development, transportation, environment, energy, and health, among others. NEGC also serves as the New England Secretariat for NEG-ECP, which first met in 1973. Through NEG-ECP, New England governors and Eastern Canadian premiers discuss issues of common interest and concern and enact policy resolutions that call for voluntary actions by the state and provincial governments and by the two national governments.[5]

NEG-ECP established the NICE in 1978 to monitor and act upon common energy issues in the New England-Eastern Canadian region. The NEG-ECP Committee on the Environment and NICE then appointed a Climate Change Steering Committee to oversee implementation of the NEG-ECP Climate Change Action Plan.

1.2.2 Climate Change Action Plan

The NEG-ECP Climate Change Action Plan identifies steps to address those aspects of climate change that are within the region's control in order to reduce regional GHG emissions, adopt adaptive measures, and build the foundation for a long-term shift to cleaner, more efficient, economically competitive, and secure ways of using energy. The Climate Change Steering Committee oversees the implementation of the action plan and reports to the Committee on the Environment and NICE on a regular basis. Both of these committees report annually to NEG-ECP.

Specifically, NEG-ECP created the action plan to:

- Provide a comprehensive and coordinated regional plan for reducing GHG through regional initiatives.
- Obtain and build commitment from each state and provincial jurisdiction to carry out its own planning for GHG reductions, including disclosure of progress and sharing of information.
- Develop a plan to adapt the region's economic resource base and physical infrastructure to the impacts of climate change.
- Develop a public education and outreach effort to ensure that the region's citizens continue to be educated about climate change.
- Maintain and enhance energy reliability and security.
- Promote sustainable economic development.

The action plan also recommends strategies to reduce regional GHG emissions cost effectively while advancing other important regional objectives – what NEG-ECP labels as a "win-win"

---

[5] Source: http://www.newenglandgovernors.org/.

solution, where all parties view quantitative and qualitative benefits as greater than costs. Other regional objectives include:

- Reducing emissions of pollutants that threaten human health and the natural environment.
- Maintaining a reliable supply of reasonably priced energy within the region.
- Reducing regional dependence on energy imports, thereby keeping energy dollars in the regional economy.
- Reducing the region's collective vulnerability to energy price shocks.
- Providing "early adoption" of innovative opportunities to enhance the competitive advantage of the region's technology industries and research.

The action plan builds on discussions held at the NEG-ECP Climate Change Workshop in March 2001. At the workshop, participants identified the following nine steps each jurisdiction or the entire region will take and incorporated these steps into the action plan:

1. Establish a standardized emissions inventory beginning with 1990 GHG emissions levels and report updates every three years.
2. Create a plan identifying measures to achieve GHG reductions through regional short and mid-term targets.
3. By 2005, make the public in the region aware of the impacts of climate change and what personal actions they can take at home and work to reduce GHG emissions.
4. By 2012, reduce GHG emissions through improved energy efficiency and the reduced public sector use of carbon-based fuels by 25 percent, as measured from an established baseline.
5. By 2025, reduce the carbon dioxide (CO_2) emitted per megawatt hour of electricity use within the region by 20 percent of current emissions.
6. By 2025, increase the amount of energy saved through conservation programs (in tons of GHG gas emissions) within the region by 20 percent by encouraging residential, commercial, industrial, and institutional energy conservation. (Action Items 5 and 6 are complementary and designed to lower the overall carbon intensity of electricity production.)
7. Broaden the understanding of forecasted climate change impacts and plan for the adaptation of these impacts, where possible. In addition, seek adaptation options that do not increase GHG emissions further.
8. Slow the growth rate of and reduce GHG emissions from transportation and better understand the impacts of transportation programs and projects on overall GHG emissions. Work with federal officials to improve the energy efficiency of vehicles for sale to the public.
9. Create a uniform and coordinated basis for GHG emissions banking and trading. Create a regional GHG emissions registry and gain experience in certifying credits and trading within the geographic region. To accomplish this, states and provinces will allow industries, organizations, and other entities to disclose their current GHG emissions baseline without being penalized for early reductions.

The Climate Change Action Plan expects each state and province to initiate a coordinated set of policies and actions aimed at advancing their common goals. The region has three benchmarks or performance measures to measure its degree of success in addressing the action plan's nine goals:[6]

- **Short-term Measure.** Reduce regional GHG emissions to 1990 emissions by 2010.

- **Mid-term Measure.** Reduce regional GHG emissions by at least 10 percent below 1990 emissions by 2020. Beginning in 2005, establish an iterative, 5-year process to adjust the goals if necessary and to set future emissions reduction goals.

- **Long-term Measure.** Reduce regional GHG emissions sufficiently to eliminate any dangerous threat to the climate. Current science suggests that this will require reductions of 75-85 percent below current levels.

Beyond these measures, each jurisdiction can choose additional measures to contribute towards meeting overall GHG reduction targets.

At the time of this report, Vermont, Maine, and Rhode Island had formally adopted their own climate change action plans. Connecticut, Massachusetts, and New Hampshire are at various stages of developing plans and should be finished in 2003. Figure 2 shows which states have adopted a climate change action plan and how these plans relate to the regional efforts of NEG-ECP and NICE.

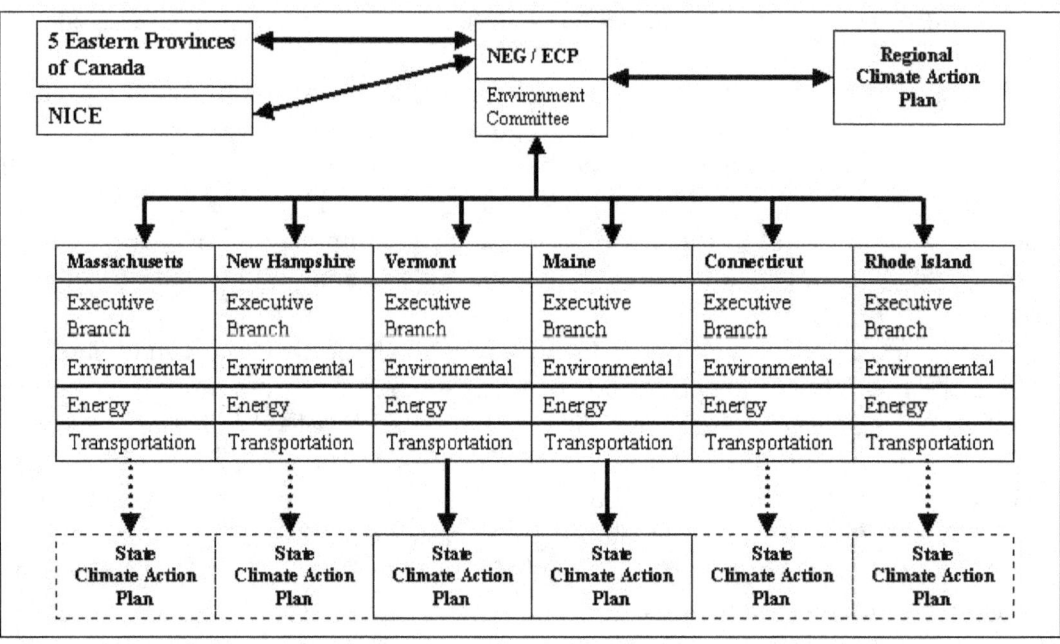

Figure 2. Climate Change Linkages for Planning Activities in New England[7]

---

[6] Note that these goals represent reductions that would need to be taken more universally, including outside the region, to have the intended positive results.

[7] Source: USDOT/Volpe Center, 2002.

1.3 Links to the Energy and Transportation Planning Process

NEG-ECP is focused on energy and efficiency, leaving the states to develop and implement policies as they see appropriate. States vary greatly in their resources and priorities, including on which sectors they choose to focus – energy or transportation.

1.3.1 Energy Planning

NICE and five of the six New England states have energy plans that allow linkages between initiatives to reduce GHG emissions and energy plans and policies.

NICE

In July 2000, NEG-ECP adopted Resolution 25-12, which directs NICE to perform the following actions to help plan for energy use and to determine reduction strategies for the energy sector:

- Continue to monitor developments in energy markets.
- Send a letter to the Secretary of the U.S. Department of Energy (DOE) recommending that DOE work with NICE, states, and provinces to maintain an open North American energy market and to clarify the treatment of large-scale hydro-electric power under federal restructuring legislation.
- Examine ways to encourage energy conservation, demand-side management programs, energy efficiency, and the development of new energy technologies.
- Continue to develop a computerized energy database for the region.
- Report on key jurisdictional energy issues in the region, including the region's energy storage capacity and infrastructure.

While NEG-ECP and NICE cooperatively developed the Climate Change Action Plan, they did not directly link the action plan and NICE's energy plan. In addition, neither group identified national or international agencies to enforce the policies or suggestions in these plans. Nonetheless, the support and advice NICE provides is an important first step in developing a regional energy plan.

Connecticut

In its Act Studying State Energy Policies (SA 99-15), the Connecticut General Assembly charged the Connecticut Board of Energy with updating and strengthening the state's energy policy.[8] The act charged the board with accomplishing the following objectives:

- Reflect emerging competition among the various public utility industries and emerging trends in new technologies.
- Repeal or modify elements of the current policy that are inconsistent with recent state and federal laws.

---

[8] Source: http://www.cga.state.ct.us/ps99/act/sa/1999sa-00015-r00sb-01285-sa htm.

- Protect the interests of low-income consumers and ensure they benefit from new opportunities available through competition, such as aggregation.
- Ensure that conservation of natural resources remains a high priority in the state's energy policy.

After establishing the energy policy's goals, Connecticut established a set of 15 energy policy strategies, as shown in Table 1. These strategies outline the ways through which the goals can best be achieved in the context of current energy conditions and markets.[9] Although Connecticut recommended that future policies support efforts to address climate change, at the time of this report the state did not appear to link the energy plan directly with the climate change action plan currently under development.

Table 1. Energy Policies for the State of Connecticut[10]

Energy Policy Strategies	Energy Policy Goals				
	A. Economic	B. Environmental	C. Risk Mitigation	D. Competitive Markets	E. Policy Coordination
(1) Monitor Retail Energy Market Development	*			*	
(2) Encourage Interstate & Federal Action to Enhance Regional Market Development				*	*
(3) Remove Barriers to Distributed Energy		*	*	*	
(4) Support Emerging & Renewable Energy Technologies		*	*	*	
(5) Protect the Interests of All Customers, Including Low-Income Customers	*				
(6) Support & Coordinate Energy Conservation and Efficiency Programs		*	*		
(7) Review Tax Incentives for Energy Efficiency and Clean Energy		*	*		
(8) Enhance Regional Supply Portfolio Diversity			*		
(9) Assess Natural Gas Restructuring	*			*	
(10) Support Adequate Levels of Fuel Storage	*		*	*	
(11) Coordinate Environmental and Energy Policies		*			*
(12) Prioritize Energy Use in Transportation and Land Use Planning			*		*
(13) Stimulate Commercialization of High-Mileage and Alternate-Fuel Vehicles	*				*
(14) Initiate a Coordinated Energy Education Campaign					*
(15) Establish an Ongoing Energy Planning Review Process					*

Maine

The Maine Office of Planning is developing and implementing a statewide clean energy agenda. The agenda emphasizes renewable energy resources and includes the following priorities:

- Reform the current renewable portfolio standard.

---
[9] Source: http://dep.state.ct.us/wst/p2/energy/energy.htm.
[10] Source: "Connecticut DRAFT Energy Plan."

- Implement a program of customer credits to spur purchases of clean energy.
- Target tax incentives to mitigate some of the barriers and costs faced by renewable energy generators.
- Promote transmission pricing and policy reforms at the regional level.

Maine's energy plan includes environmental and climate change concerns and defines energy's role in the state's 1996 climate change action plan.

Massachusetts

The Massachusetts Legislature created the Renewable Energy Trust in 1998 to restructure the electric utility industry and to promote the development of renewable energy in the commonwealth. In keeping with its legislative mandate, the Trust focuses on four statutory objectives:

- Shift electric energy consumption in Massachusetts from conventional energy resources to a greater reliance on energy generated from renewable resources.
- Increase electric generating capacity from renewable resources to meet the growing energy demands of consumers in Massachusetts.
- Expand the renewable energy sector in Massachusetts, including system developers, manufacturers, equipment vendors, architects and engineers, service providers, and research organizations.
- Increase the overall level of economic activity related to renewable energy in the commonwealth.

Massachusetts cited the environment as a concern in the state's energy plan and is currently developing a climate change action plan. The extent to which these plans will be linked is unknown.

New Hampshire

New Hampshire is currently developing energy and climate change action plans that will share common objectives. It is not yet known whether they will be linked.

Rhode Island

The Rhode Island Council adopted a state energy plan on March 13, 1997. Developed by an interdisciplinary subcommittee of public and private sector experts, the plan identifies key energy issues and establishes related policies and actions. The overall objective of the plan is to ensure a supply of energy that is reliable, low-cost, environmentally benign, sufficient for economic growth, and safe from supply disruptions. The subcommittee has identified several goals and strategies in the plan, including the following:

- State policy should encourage the direct use of natural gas in end-uses determined to be economically and environmentally appropriate, especially those which help reduce the demand for electricity during summer and winter peak demand periods.
- State policy should encourage the move toward true electricity competition via regional cooperation and planning.
- State policy should support the expansion of natural gas pipeline capacity into the region and state to promote fuel diversity for direct end-use applications and electricity generation.
- State policy should continue to reduce dependence on oil through conservation and the enhancement of fuel diversity.
- State policy should stimulate the introduction of new technologies that include wind, solar, and fuel cells to provide new capacity as needed. State policy should also stimulate the creation of methods that decrease resistance in both electrical motors and transmission lines so as to increase efficiency.

The Rhode Island State Energy Plan cites numerous policies that promote energy conservation and environmental protection but does not mention climate change or GHG emissions. Rhode Island is in the process of developing a climate change action plan; it is not yet apparent whether this plan will be linked to its energy plan.

Vermont

Vermont's energy plan, "Fueling Vermont's Future," presents "bold new policies for sound energy use."[11] The state has taken action in the following areas:

- Capturing more energy savings in existing homes and businesses.
- Increasing the use of renewable energy sources.
- Improving transportation energy use. (Transportation is the largest energy user in Vermont.)
- Reviewing energy policy and taxation at the state and federal levels to ensure that energy goals are promoted.

All of the New England states have begun considering energy planning, most have begun to examine climate change issues, and some have directly linked their energy and climate change plans into one document. However, others have yet to make these connections. Level of involvement and commitment appears to vary substantially state to state.

1.3.2   Transportation Planning

NEG-ECP left the development of transportation policies related to climate change up to the states. As with energy planning, the states are at different levels of involvement and commitment in linking transportation planning with climate change policies. In general, the states do not appear to explicitly refer to climate change in their transportation plans.

---

[11] Source: http://www.state.vt.us/psd/DPSLibrary/cepGuide.htm.

Connecticut

According to the Connecticut Environmental Protection Department's 1998 emissions inventory, the transportation sector contributes over 36 percent of all GHG emissions in the state. The Connecticut DOT includes climate change concerns in its 2001 transportation plan and identifies transportation strategies to improve the environment and the mobility of people. The Connecticut DOT identified the following selection of transportation initiatives as a way of improving air quality and the environment.

- Offering incentives to encourage drivers of single-occupancy vehicles to use mass transit or carpools. (Nearly 75 percent of the state's drivers travel solo to work.)
- Improving the quality, quantity, and ease of accessing buses, trains, and light rail.
- Simplifying the transfer between different modes.
- Reducing the volume of tractor-trailers on Interstates 95, 91, and 84 by a variety of means such as increasing weight limits and improving railroad freight services. The state's waterways, in particular the Long Island Sound, remain unutilized corridors for reducing freight traffic and minimizing truck emissions.
- Establishing transit links among New Haven; Hartford; Bradley International Airport; and Springfield, Massachusetts.
- Expanding air service into Tweed in order to reduce vehicle miles traveled and automobile emissions.

Because Connecticut did not have a climate change action plan at the time of this review, it was not possible to determine direct linkages between transportation planning and climate change policies.

Maine

The transportation sector contributes almost half (47 percent) of Maine's GHG emissions. Increasing amounts of vehicle miles traveled (VMT) and the current fuel efficiency of vehicles significantly affects CO_2 emissions from the transportation sector. As part of their overall policy to improve transportation service and air quality, the state identified several policy actions:

- Implementing Maine DOT transportation plans that maximize emissions reductions programs.
- Working with municipalities and developers to promote efficient patterns of development that reduce VMT.
- Establishing a system of bikeways and public transit vans.
- Marketing public transit to citizens.
- Promoting the benefits of ridesharing in cars and vans.
- Enacting a "feebate program" to charge for the use of gas-guzzling vehicles.
- Supporting the Clean Cities Program.
- Working with the Maine DOT to utilize TEA-21 legislation.

- Working with Congress to reform the corporate average fuel economy (CAFE) standards.

Vermont

Vermont's Climate Change Action Plan states that transportation planning and policies offer the greatest opportunities for increasing energy efficiency and for reducing GHG emissions and reliance on oil. Vermont has proposed several strategies and policies that would implement least cost transportation planning and broaden the focus of transportation planning in order to access a wide variety of resources at the lowest cost to society. The strategies and policies related to transportation include:

- Reducing VMT and transportation-related emissions.
- Using transportation energy taxation to remove market distortions from energy prices and "internalize" more of the societal and environmental costs into transportation fuel prices.
- Using a "feebate" program to recognize that efficient vehicles impose lower costs and impacts than less efficient, gas-guzzling vehicles.
- Increasing the efficiency of vehicles through higher CAFE standards and state polices that maximize fuel efficiency and minimize safety risks and associated emergency service costs.
- Continuing the implementation of vapor recovery at gas stations and adopting a low emissions vehicle standard.
- Implementing policies that shift travel to more efficient modes of transportation, including buses, vanpools, trains, and non-motorized transportation.
- Promoting telecommuting.

1.4   Lessons Learned

NEG-ECP provides a forum for the governors of New England to coordinate and implement policies and programs designed to respond to regional issues, including GHG emissions reduction and climate change. In its regional climate change action plan, NEG-ECP focused on energy. At the same time, each New England state is developing its own climate change action plan and linking transportation and energy policies to different degrees. The Canadian provinces, Vermont, and Maine have made noteworthy early progress in developing plans that link energy and transportation planning. In general, continued political support will be essential for these links to be expanded and strengthened.

This research identified several key lessons learned:

- **Directly linking climate change policies to other policies, such as air quality and energy, may provide synergistic benefits.** Directly linking these policies demonstrates the interrelationships between climate change, energy, environment, economics, and transportation. This direct linkage can also demonstrate that actions that further one goal can further others, encouraging political support.

- **Political support on a broad geographical basis is necessary.** Climate change issues have no borders. Acknowledging this fact is a critical first step towards developing cooperation and political support across state lines and international boundaries. The challenge is to turn this awareness and support into actual policies and initiatives that can be implemented by national, state, and local jurisdictions.

- **Regional approaches encourage participation and action.** NEG-ECP's success at raising awareness demonstrates how a regional approach can establish a visible and high-profile forum for political leaders and governments to exchange ideas, provide mutual encouragement, and develop coordinated climate change policies.

- **Regional workshops foster understanding.** Workshops and seminars at the regional level help stakeholders understand climate change issues and work cooperatively to develop solutions.

- **Beginning to formulate a "win-win" approach can provide a useful foundation for policy development.** NEG-ECP began its climate change policy development by attempting to formulate a "win-win" approach that required minimal financial and political investment and produced easily identifiable and cost-effective results. This kind of approach can provide the foundation for later, more complex efforts and can encourage early cooperation.

- **A broad-based coalition can provide a laboratory for ideas.** As a multistate and multiprovince initiative, NEG-ECP provides a laboratory for studying policies and strategies in a broad range of situations. The region has had experience assessing the following ideas:
  - "Feebate" programs for gas-guzzling vehicles in rural areas with a high proportion of trucks and utility vehicles.
  - Reform of CAFE standards to address climate change in rural areas with a large proportion of trucks traveling long distances, such as in Maine.
  - Combination energy and climate change action plans that support an efficient and coordinated approach to addressing issues, such as in Vermont.

2. NEW JERSEY

2.1 Introduction

New Jersey's approach to reducing GHG emissions has been shaped by its industrial base and geography. New Jersey is geographically vulnerable to the impacts of climate change: the state is surrounded on three sides by water. In the mid-1990s, the New Jersey Coastline Study increased concerns about sea-level rise due to climate change. As a result, New Jersey feels compelled to take strong and collaborative actions to reduce GHG emissions. Initially, former New Jersey Governor Christine Todd Whitman and former New Jersey Department of Environmental Protection (NJDEP) Commissioner Robert Shinn identified air pollution caused by industrialization and sea level rise caused by climate change as two of the most significant problems affecting the state. Over time, climate change is expected to melt ice fields, raise regional sea levels, and increase coastal flooding. Former Governor Whitman became concerned that the state's tourism industry, ecosystems, natural resources, and residential communities would be threatened. Former Commissioner Shinn described New Jersey's vulnerability at a press conference for the state's Sustainability Initiatives, which link climate change to air pollution, health problems, and economic woes:

> If sea levels continue to rise and intense flooding occurs as predicted, our environment and our economy will suffer. In addition, warmer weather means more summertime smog and pollution, endangering the health of young children, those who work or exercise outdoors, the elderly, and especially persons with asthma or other respiratory problems.[12]

In June 1997, New Jersey formed a climate change working group comprised of representatives from NJDEP, New Jersey Department of Transportation (NJDOT), eight other state agencies, two federal agencies, and several key external stakeholders. The working group developed a plan of options to reduce GHG emissions. In March 1998, New Jersey became the first state to establish a statewide goal for GHG reductions, according to local sources. The state outlined strategies and milestones to meet these goals in its April 2000 "Sustainability Greenhouse Gas Action Plan" (SGGAP).

2.2 Approach

New Jersey is taking a "no regrets" and "low hanging fruit" approach to addressing climate change: initially, the state is only planning and developing environmentally beneficial and cost-effective programs and policies that it believes can be achieved with minimal political and financial effort. This practical approach allows NJDEP to show early results to elected officials and the public and to establish momentum for future policy considerations.

New Jersey included several key components in its master plan to reduce GHG emissions:

- Use government officials to heighten awareness and educate citizens and businesses.
- Develop specific strategies for each sector of the economy.
- Create an inventory of GHG emissions.
- Develop more detailed estimates on fuel use statewide.
- Improve the research tools that could be used to evaluate policy options.
- Support projects that explore innovative energy technologies that emit less GHG.

Based on this master plan, New Jersey first inventoried its GHG emissions for 1990 to understand the extent of its climate change problems. That year, New Jersey emitted approximately 130 million metric tons of GHG, or about two percent of the nation's GHG emissions. More then 80 percent of those emissions came from the combustion of fossil fuels to produce energy. If left unchecked, GHG emissions were expected to grow to over 150 million metric tons by 2005. Figure 3 shows GHG emissions by major sector: transportation, residential, commercial, and industrial.

---

[12] Source: http://www.state.nj.us/dep/newsrel/releases/00_0030.htm.

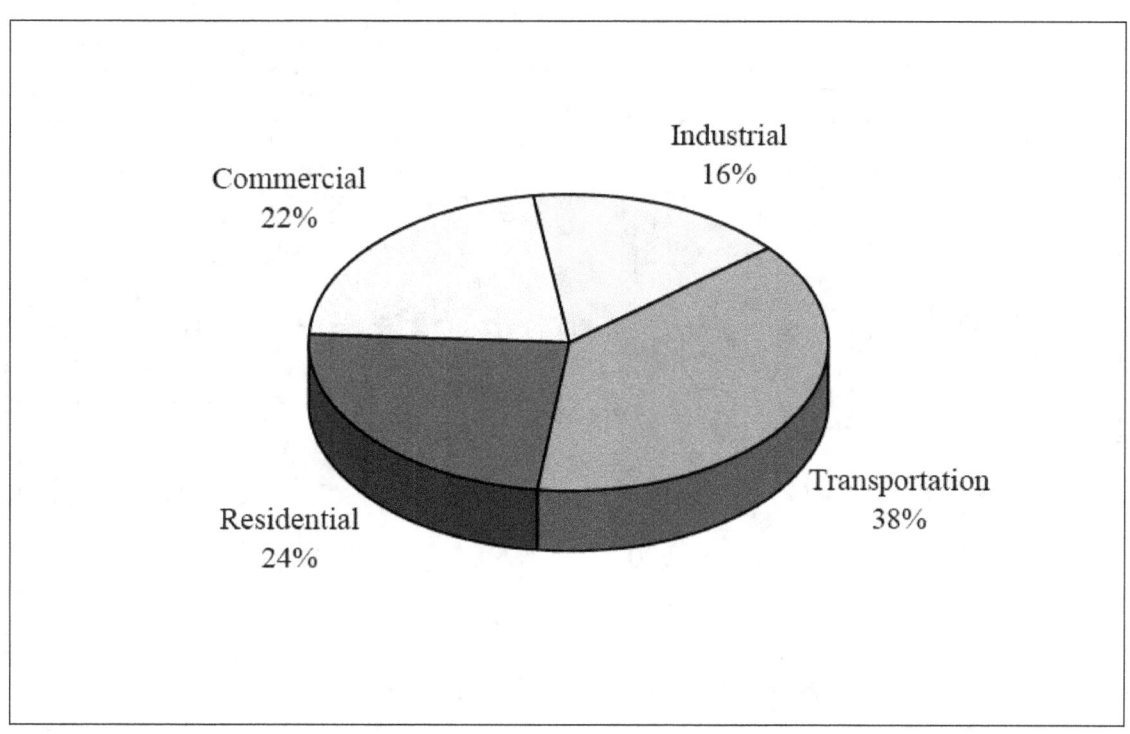

Figure 3. GHG Emissions by Sector, 1990 New Jersey Emissions Inventory[13]

Next, New Jersey evaluated the feasibility of reducing GHG emissions at a variety of levels over the next five years. After consulting with the working group, NJDEP established a GHG emissions reduction goal of 3.5 percent below 1990 levels by 2005. To meet this goal, New Jersey will reduce 20 million tons of CO_2 from 1997 levels, as indicated in Figure 4.

---

[13] Source: "White Paper on Global Climate Change in NJ: Milestones & Indicators," 2000.

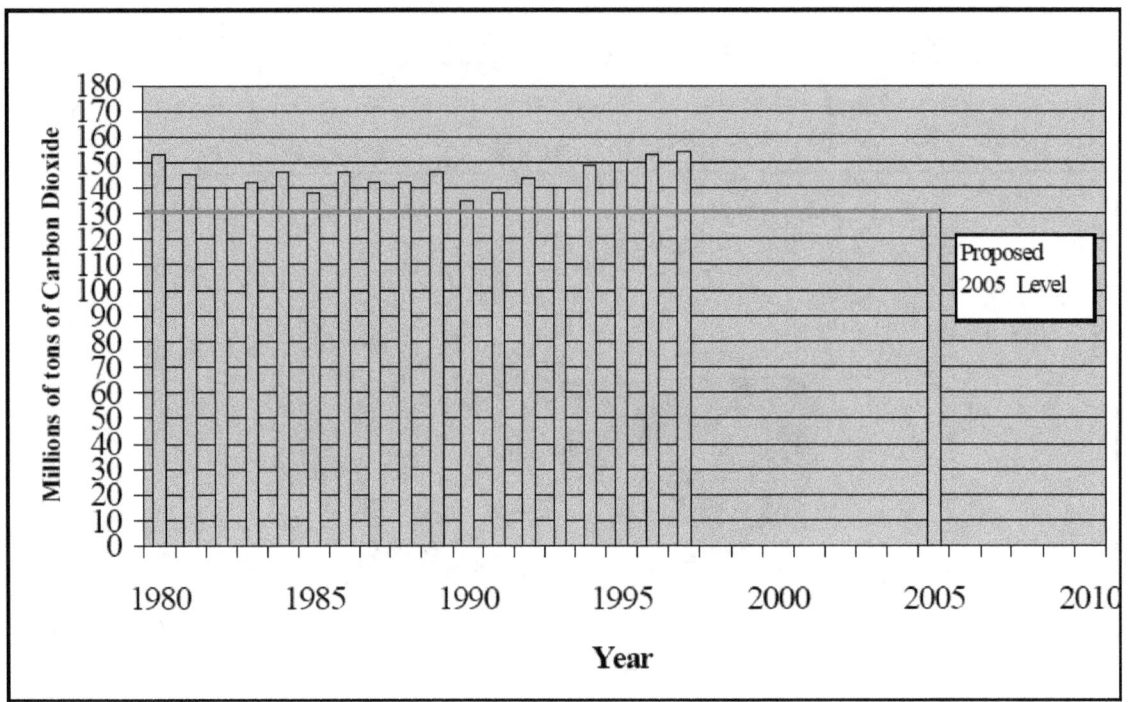

Figure 4. New Jersey GHG Emissions and Target Level[14]

To help promote GHG reduction effort at the state level, former Governor Whitman directed all state agencies to pursue the goals outlined in the 1999 report "Living With the Future in Mind – Goals and Indicators for NJ Quality of Life."[15] Former Governor Whitman also directed all state agencies to share information and establish institutional mechanisms that encourage and facilitate the sustainability goals outlined in the report. NJDEP outlined strategies and methods for meeting these goals in the SGGAP. Through its strategic plan and the National Environmental Performance Partnership System (NEPPS), NJDEP developed specific GHG indicators to track the progress in using the SGGAP strategies.

2.2.1 Who Is Involved and Why

Since 1997, NJDEP has organized the state's efforts to address climate change and worked with a variety of stakeholders, including federal, state, and local government agencies, businesses, utilities, non-profit groups, academia, and citizens. To help implement the SGGAP, NJDEP enlisted the aid of as many stakeholders as possible to accomplish early results, including voluntarily contributing to the 3.5 percent GHG reduction goal by signing a "Covenant of Sustainability." Initially, NJDEP emphasized emissions reductions from the biggest GHG contributors in the state – businesses and utilities. NJDEP is now focusing on schools and county governments. Finally, NJDEP will focus on the transportation sector.

Among state agencies, NJDEP, the New Jersey Treasury Department, and the New Jersey Department of Community Affairs are the most active in implementing the state's climate

---

[14] Source: "NJ Sustainability GHG Action Plan," 1999 – adapted by the USDOT/Volpe Center.
[15] New Jersey Future, a non-profit and non-partisan group, developed this document as a report card on the long-term trends that can enhance or diminish the quality of life in New Jersey.

change initiative. Other state agencies, including NJDOT, have been less actively involved. Many agencies have signed the Covenant of Sustainability but still are identifying strategies to implement. At the local level, a number of communities signed the covenant, while at the federal level, the Environmental Protection Agency (EPA) and the DOE are providing financial support. In 2001, a number of government, industry, and environmental groups signed the covenant. By voluntarily participating in the SGGAP, these organizations identify themselves publicly as environmentally aware and concerned and project a positive image that is helpful for marketing. Three non-profit agencies endorsed but did not sign the covenant – Natural Resource Defense Council, Environmental Defense, and New Jersey Future.

2.2.2 The Climate Protection Plan

Sustainability Greenhouse Gas Action Plan Strategies
• Energy Conservation • Innovative Technologies • Innovative Research • Pollution Prevention • Waste Management • Natural Resources-Open Space • Outreach & Education

The report "Living With the Future in Mind" provided the groundwork for the SGGAP and identified 11 goals and 41 indicators to measure progress towards meeting those goals. Two of these goals – reducing energy consumption and reducing GHG emissions – are particularly vital to the SGGAP.

The SGGAP identified goals, objectives, baseline conditions, strategies, and methods to monitor the plan's success. The baseline was developed using two approaches: identifying survey data from the DOE and the Energy Information Agency (EIA) and using data supplied by the EPA. The goal of the plan is to achieve a 3.5 percent reduction in GHG emissions, specifically CO_2 emissions, using the "no regrets" approach. Specific techniques to meet the strategies identified in the SGGAP include improved fuel efficiency, greater use of mass transit and energy efficient appliances, more efficient commercial and residential heating/cooling systems, increased use of fuel cells, greater recycling, and tree planting.

Former Governor Whitman earmarked $320,000 in the FY01 budget to implement the SGGAP. Through NEPPS, NJDEP identified milestones and measures to track progress, as shown in Table 2. NJDEP reports annually on the state's progress in implementing SGGAP's strategies.

Other Groups that Signed the Covenant of Sustainability, New Jersey (partial list)
• Cosmair, Inc. – Clark manufacturing • DuPont Chambers Works • Johnson & Johnson • Lucent Technologies • Philips Lighting Company • Jersey Central Power & Light – GPU Energy • PSEE&G • Schools

Table 2. Milestones and Measures to Track Progress in New Jersey[16]

	Milestone	Measure
1	Total GHG Emissions	Indirect - Using DOE EIA Data
2	Commutation by Public Transportation	VMT and Trips Recorded
3	Sea Level Rise	Sea Level at Atlantic City
4	Surface Air Temperature	Statewide Average Temperature
5	Amount of Precipitation	Statewide Average Precipitation
6	Commercial Energy Use	Environmental Auditors Registration Association (EARA)
7	Residential Energy Use	EARA
8	Industrial Energy Use	EARA
9	Government Energy Use	EARA

2.3 Links to the Planning Process

SGGAP goals are incorporated into NJDEP's strategic plan, the performance partnership agreement under NEPPS, the state's development and redevelopment plan, and indirectly into several of the state MPOs' regional long-range transportation plans. NJDEP is now working to have all state agencies signing the Covenant of Sustainability. At the local level, NJDEP is recruiting MPOs and counties to voluntarily commit to the strategies identified in the SGGAP. Figure 5 identifies New Jersey's key stakeholders and linkages between climate change and transportation planning. The solid lines represent formalized communication, while the dotted lines represent less formal processes and less frequent communication.

---

[16] Source: "NJDEP Global Climate Change: Milestones & Indicators," 2000.

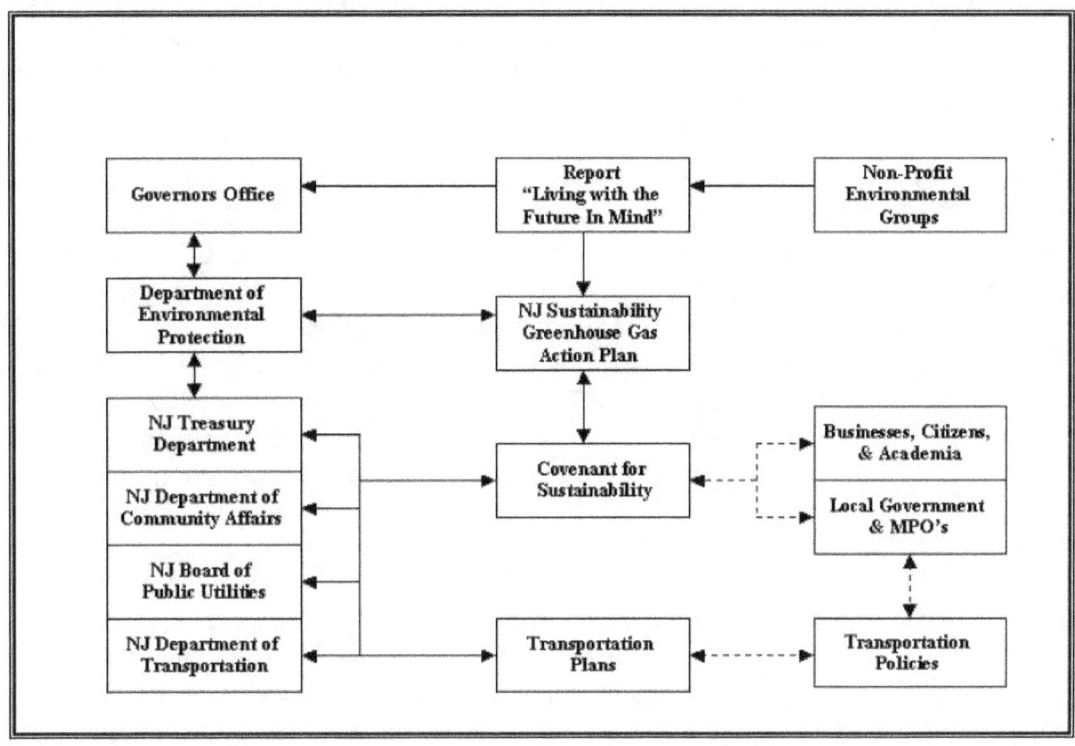

Figure 5. Climate Change Planning Process in New Jersey[17]

2.3.1 Energy Planning

New Jersey's master energy plan incorporates climate change issues. SGGAP identifies three basic policies from the energy plan:

- Generating energy using sources that produce less GHG.
- Employing more efficient means of fuel consumption.
- Capturing wasted energy for productive use.

New Jersey has developed several "energy conservation and innovative technologies" initiatives to implement these policies, including:

- Electric Discount and Energy Competition Act–Renewable Technologies Initiative.
- Renewable Technology Projects in State Parks and Other State Facilities Initiative.
- Building a Greener New Jersey Partnership.
- Sustainable Development/Affordable Housing Pilot Program.
- Sustainable Development Loan Fund.
- Million Solar Roof State and Local Partnership.

---

[17] Source: USDOT/Volpe Center, 2002.

While the energy plan and the SGGAP share some of the same goals, the New Jersey agencies developed the plans at different times. As a result, linkages to the planning process may be limited. In addition, the energy plan proposes solutions but does not appear to provide detail as to who will implement them or how.

2.3.2 Transportation Planning

SGGAP identifies several transportation planning initiatives that NJDOT is implementing to meet the 2005 reduction goal. These initiatives fall into three approaches – regulatory, operations, and research – and focus on increasing the fuel efficiency of vehicles, providing incentives for people and businesses to use alternative fuels or modes of transportation, and establishing supportive infrastructure. NJDOT is applying the same "no regrets" approach as NJDEP. These initiatives may or may not have explicit GHG impacts, and estimates of projected GHG emissions reductions resulting from these strategies were not available.

NJDOT Transportation Planning Initiatives

Regulatory

- Require that transportation strategies be implemented to improve air quality and comply with the Clean Air Act.
- Implement an enhanced vehicle inspection and maintenance program. A new bi-yearly inspection program could identify up to 4 percent of on-the-road vehicles with serious emissions problems, resulting in a 10 percent improvement in GHG emissions for these vehicles.
- Work with the DOE to require that municipal and private fleets comply with federal Energy Policy Act (EPAct) legislation. Created in 1992, EPAct improves environmental quality by managing energy demand and supply. The program requires federal fleets to increase fuel efficiency and convert to alternative fuels.
- Require that the New Jersey Clean Fleet Program and its centrally fueled fleets of ten or more vehicles participate in climate change initiatives. (Currently, the program is voluntary.)
- Support legislation, such as the Comprehensive Alternative Motor Fuel Promotion Act (A646), that uses tax incentives to support infrastructure development that supports alternative fuels.
- Foster interagency collaboration to ensure that New Jersey's new vehicle contract includes standards that require fuel-efficient vehicles and the consideration of Alternative Fuel Vehicles (AFV).
- Require all state duel fueled vehicles to operate at least 25 percent of the time on clean burning fuels.

<u>Operations</u>

- Support mass transit improvements, such as a new Amtrak station in Hamilton and a new light rail service from Camden. The state believes that new stations could decrease VMT and GHG emissions, as discussed in the 1999 New Jersey Sustainability Report.
- Develop a 5-year AFV plan in cooperation with other agencies. According to the plan, this will allow New Jersey to fund, implement, manage, and monitor AFV fleets.
- Reduce the state vehicle fleet by a fixed percentage each year.
- Expand the Alternative Fuel Demonstration Project, which is using electric vehicles in state parks.
- Develop an alternative fuel infrastructure that includes refueling and maintenance sites.

<u>Research</u>

- Support research to improve alternative fuels such as electricity, natural gas, hybrid fuels, and fuel cells.
- Support research to develop a low emissions vehicle program that would reduce vehicle emissions.

New Jersey's efforts to reduce GHG emissions from the transportation sector is evolving. The state hopes that each participating agency will incorporate voluntary climate change commitments into its long-range strategic plans. However, many agencies are struggling to find ways to incorporate these voluntary commitments into the planning documents without undermining regulatory requirements that are already in place.

2.4 Results to Date

New Jersey's early progress appears to be significant. According to the state, it reduced CO_2 emissions from all sectors by 1.8 million metric tons from the baseline through its energy efficiency initiatives in 2001. New Jersey also reduced emissions of other GHG, including nitrous oxides (NO_x), and sulfur dioxide (SO_2), as shown in Table 3. New Jersey is now capitalizing on these early successes to help build more support for its climate change initiatives.

CO_2 Reductions by Sector for New Jersey (2001)
• Residential: 97,000 metric tons
• Commercial/Industrial: 1.7 million metric tons

Table 3. Emissions Savings Reported in 2001: Statewide Summary for New Jersey (Reported in Metric Tons) [18]

Program by Sector	CO_2	NO_x	SO_2	Mercury
Residential Energy Efficiency: Electric	52,800	154	246	0.0012
Residential Energy Efficiency: Low Income Loans	36,800	107	172	0.0008
Residential Energy Efficiency: New Construction	7,100	21	33	0.0002
Commercial/Industrial Efficiency	1,728,200	5,043	8,060	0.0393
Total Savings	**1,824,900**	**5,325**	**8,511**	**0.0415**

2.5   How the Process Has Evolved

Industrialization and state geography turned climate change into a high priority for former Governor Whitman. New Jersey used the New Jersey Coastal Study and a 1990 GHG emissions inventory to quantitatively assess the problem. NJDEP then created and began implementing the SGGAP by identifying stakeholders and by educating and enlisting the support of the public and the private sector. Initially targeting utilities and businesses, NJDEP used the Covenant of Sustainability to promote SGGAP in order to get the quickest and biggest return. NJDEP's initial efforts included energy conservation and efficiency initiatives. To build voluntary support and encourage early adapter, NJDEP showcased those companies and agencies that signed on early to the Covenant of Sustainability.

New Jersey's climate change process evolved as three issues were explored:

- The new governor's approach to the climate change issue.
- Whether the "no regrets strategy" can evolve to include initiatives with clear abilities to reduce GHG emissions but more challenging political or financial implications.
- Continued progress in the annual updates toward the 3.5 percent reduction goal.

Through these early efforts, New Jersey has laid the political groundwork necessary to explore new policies and initiatives that move beyond the early focus of energy efficiency. New Jersey's new administration will determine future progress, including fostering energy savings in the transportation sector. Continued support will help extend the focus on energy savings in the residential, commercial, and industrial sectors to include other sources like transportation. Support for current and future initiatives will depend on continuous political support and ability to identify and promote cost-effective policies.

---

[18] Source: "SGGAP 2001 NJDEP, Addendum."

2.6   Lessons Learned

Changing the transportation planning process to reflect climate change concerns and reduce CO_2 emissions is a complex process. There may be political or regulatory factors that states or metropolitan areas should consider to enable GHG emissions reductions to be reflected in their long-range transportation plans. For example, transportation planners may be concerned that introducing a GHG emissions reduction goal might add expectations or technical considerations that might make it more difficult to meet air conformity requirements. In this case, the state might consider how transportation planning might introduce goals to reduce GHG emissions without making it more difficult to meet air quality conformity requirements. One possible solution might be to reflect GHG reduction goals as part of a vision component of state or MPO transportation plans, allowing climate change goals and reduction strategies to be considered without creating difficulties for meeting air conformity requirements. Success and innovation in New Jersey on this issue could be helpful to other states and metropolitan areas.

This research identified several key lessons learned:

- **"Champions" play a critical role.** The early support of former Commissioner Shinn and former Governor Whitman were critical to the success of New Jersey's early climate change initiatives.

- **Focusing on impacts can promote strategies.** By identifying climate change-related problems and impacts early, New Jersey was able to promote its related strategies.

- **An initial "no regrets" approach can foster momentum.** By following a "no regrets" approach in the beginning, New Jersey implemented early successes that could be quantified, quickly accomplished, and shown to stakeholders as cost effective and environmentally beneficial. New Jersey's approach helped establish the early political support needed to build momentum for future initiatives.

- **Linking to energy efficiency plans can reduce GHG emissions from the baseline.** Reducing energy consumption from the residential, commercial, and industrial sectors through energy efficiency outreach, education, and voluntary commitments provided substantial GHG emission reductions.

- **Voluntary programs encourage participation.** The Covenant for Sustainability provided a positive marketing incentive for the numerous government agencies and business that signed it, and encouraged other constituencies to participate.   The Covenant is a tool to encourage public and private entities to commit to reductions. It provides a basis for these groups to market their innovative ideas and allows the state to track commitments by businesses, utilities, and schools.

- **Targeting sectors with large GHG emissions provides early results.** New Jersey began its GHG reduction efforts by identifying the largest sectors contributing to GHG emissions and then encouraging their involvement in reduction efforts. To target the energy sector, NJDEP focused first on the utility industry, which was interested in participating and could demonstrate important reductions. This focus on "low hanging fruit" allowed New Jersey to create early momentum.

- **Special incentive programs foster participation.** New Jersey provided incentives to businesses to reduce or prevent GHG emissions. Through its energy discount, Energy Competition Act, and Societal Benefits Program, New Jersey encouraged utilities to reinvest in alternative energy sources. In addition, New Jersey linked environmental performance with regulatory oversight in its Silver Track II Program. The program provides regulatory flexibility to companies with superior track records in GHG emissions reductions. All of these programs spur reductions in GHG emission, encourage energy conservation, and build a foundation for expansion.

- **Incorporating GHG goals into transportation planning can be a challenge.** New Jersey began with initial successes with industries, utilities, and other businesses, next turning to local governments and schools. The state is now focusing on the transportation sector, labeled by a New Jersey contact as particularly challenging. Other areas may find it useful to consider how to include GHG goals conceptually, such as within a vision component in state or metropolitan 20-year transportation plans. Addressing GHG goals conceptually in transportation planning may help to gain public and political interest and to demonstrate interactions between climate change and transportation policies and related large-scale trade-offs.

3. DELAWARE

3.1 Introduction

Delaware has several years of detailed experience in statewide GHG emissions reduction planning and approaches the issue from both smart growth and energy perspectives. The state has actively involved major corporations, university research centers, state and local government agencies, and non-profit organizations, and the quality of communication among the various groups has contributed to producing a climate change action plan that is widely accepted and influential, in particular as a framework for a statewide energy plan.

The climate change action plan is noteworthy because of the sectoral breadth of the membership of the consortium that developed it. Consortium members were committed long-term to GHG reduction generally and to the climate change action plan specifically. The recommendations put forward in the plan were based on rigorous technical analysis by sector and were reached through a consensus-based decision-making process. These factors contributed to the widespread support and acceptance that the plan enjoys in Delaware.

While the climate change action plan has not been officially incorporated into Delaware's statewide transportation plan, representatives from the Delaware DOT (DelDOT) have been at the table throughout the plan's development. The plan's proposed transportation goals agree with the state's overall transportation vision as discussed in the current statewide transportation plan. The transportation plan was issued in 1997, before the development of the climate change action plan, and does not detail specific actions to be taken to reduce GHG emissions. However, the transportation plan is clearly influenced by Delaware's smart growth principles, and the GHG reduction goals in the climate change action plan complement overall goals and policies set forth in the transportation plan.

3.2   Approach

Delaware has several plans that address GHG emissions, including its smart growth plan, "Shaping Delaware's Future: Managing Growth in 21st Century Delaware, Strategies for State Policies and Spending," and its GHG reduction plan, "Delaware Climate Change Action Plan." The first smart growth plan reviewed for this study, which was released in 1995 and updated in 2000, provides the groundwork for efforts to reduce GHG emissions through references to transportation planning and recognition that the transportation sector contributes 24 percent of Delaware's total GHG emissions. Delaware can use this reference to transportation planning and acknowledgment of transportation's contribution to GHG emissions as first steps towards developing future specific actions.

The climate change action plan is very detailed and specific. In the plan, Delaware addresses GHG emissions in multiple sectors (industrial, residential, commercial, transportation, electric utility, and wastes and forests), details three different action scenarios to be explored within each sector, and identifies the anticipated results of each scenario in terms of reductions in GHG emissions. The scenarios, which build upon the GHG inventory supported by an earlier grant from the EPA, are labeled as "Modest Commitment," "Major Commitment," and "Full Implementation." Each scenario proposes actions to achieve specified percentage levels of reduction in baseline GHG emissions by sector and overall. As their names imply, the scenarios involve different levels of commitment and challenge in achieving the specified goals.

More recently, the momentum from the climate change action plan has been absorbed into efforts to develop a statewide energy plan. Delaware is using the climate change action plan as a framework for the proposed goals of the energy plan. The energy plan is still in its formative stages and was not available for review in time for this report.

3.2.1   Who Is Involved and Why

The Delaware State Energy Department has served as the lead agency in securing funding for developing climate change goals and action strategies, with some additional funding supplied by the University of Delaware. With this funding, Delaware formed a Climate Change Consortium, a 36-member group representing a wide cross-section of state and national agencies and operating out of the University of Delaware's Center for Energy and Environmental Policy. The consortium includes corporations, unions, environmental organizations and agencies, university groups, political entities, energy organizations and agencies, natural resources groups, economic development agencies, transportation agencies, and planning agencies. Members include:

- Delaware State Energy Office (SEO)
- Center for Energy and Environmental Policy, University of Delaware
- Delaware Department of Agriculture - Forest Service
- Delaware State Senate
- United Auto Workers Local 435
- DuPont Corporation
- Students for the Environment, University of Delaware
- U.S. EPA, Philadelphia Support Office
- Delaware Nature Society
- U.S. DOE, Philadelphia Support Office
- Delaware Division of the Public Advocate
- Office of Public Relations, University of Delaware

- Delaware Economic Development Office
- Planning Department, City of Wilmington
- Delaware Electric Cooperative
- Sun Company, Inc.
- League of Women Voters
- Civil and Environmental Engineering, University of Delaware
- Delaware Department of Natural Resources (DNR) and Environmental Control
- DelDOT
- AstroPower
- Applied Energy Group
- City of Dover

The range of groups participating in the Climate Change Consortium and the consortium's consensus-based decision-making process contributed to the broad base of support for the climate change action plan. The coordination of the consortium by the Center for Energy and Environmental Policy gave the consortium more independence than might have been the case had it been under the umbrella of an organization with specific responsibilities (e.g., for energy, environment, or transportation). Including major corporations such as the DuPont Corporation helped to ensure that proposed actions were not only politically acceptable but also corporately acceptable. DuPont has a long-standing interest in and commitment to these efforts, having been the first company to take part in the carbon trading program begun in October 2001. DuPont is working toward achieving an environmentally friendly corporate image, and local contacts believe that this image may give it a competitive edge in the global market as DuPont has a number of products, such as chemical membranes and insulation, that will benefit from an environmentally friendly market.

Consortium members tended to be personally dedicated to the climate change issue, which has encouraged the long-time commitment required of members. Members also represented agencies that were in a position to facilitate and/or hinder the planning process. The consortium's consensus-based decision-making process tended to eliminate objections that might be raised by management at members' agencies. The transparent technical econometric modeling done by university researchers also aided in building the confidence of members in the validity of anticipated research results.

Consortium members have shown impressive commitment to climate change and energy policy in Delaware, even continuing to meet after the release of the climate change action plan. According to state contacts, many of these members will likely continue to be involved by working to develop the energy plan, although this is a separate effort.

The energy plan has absorbed much of the momentum from the climate change action plan. While it is being initiated from the governor's office, development of the energy plan is being lead by the director of the Energy Department. The specific groups involved in developing this plan include:

- DelDOT
- Delaware DNR and Environmental Control
- Delaware Department of Education
- Center for Energy and Environmental Policy, University of Delaware
- Non-governmental organizations involved in research or environmental issues
- Public Service Commission

3.2.2 Climate Change Action Plan

The climate change action plan is the primary document through which Delaware is addressing GHG reductions. Delaware also has a smart growth plan, which is updated periodically. The climate change action plan appears to be widely accepted as a valid planning document and is being used as the starting point and framework for Delaware's energy plan. This coordination and linkage, and the thought processes and players that produced these plans, have the potential to produce two plans closely tied together and to provide some hope that Delaware might see real GHG reductions.

The climate change action plan built upon an existing GHG inventory. From there, University of Delaware researchers constructed econometric models to create a "Business as Usual" scenario: assuming nothing were done, the model predicts reasonable expectations for future GHG emissions levels. A variety of possible actions to reduce GHG emissions presented by consortium members were modeled to determine their likely impacts.

The emission-reducing actions were broken down by sector (industrial, residential, commercial, transportation, electric utility, and wastes and forests), and a working group was formed to address each sector. Results from the working groups were then brought to the consortium for consideration. All decisions were consensus-based; there was no voting. If one member did not feel that the group he or she represented would endorse an action, then that action was not included. The working groups also developed public outreach and education efforts. Though public outreach and education were not originally envisioned, consortium members determined that they would be essential in getting actions passed.

The consortium and researchers developed and modeled three different action plan scenarios entailing three different levels of commitment: "Full Implementation," "Major Commitment," and "Modest Commitment." Each of these scenarios involves different levels of CO_2 emissions reductions in each sector from the 1990 baseline, as shown by Table 4. These scenarios were evaluated based not only on amount of CO_2 emissions reduced, but also on cost-effectiveness, political feasibility, and environmental and mobility advantages. The consortium endorsed the "Major Commitment" scenario, which includes a 23 percent reduction in CO_2.

Table 4. Forecast 2010 Permanent Reduction in CO_2 Emissions by Energy End-Use Sector from 1990 Baseline[19]

	Modest Commitment	Major Commitment	Full Implementation
Industry	9%	18%	27%
Residential	10%	18%	28%
Commercial	9%	18%	27%
Transportation	**10%**	**24%**	**36%**
Utilities	17%	24%	40%
Total	**12%**	**23%**	**32%**

3.3 Links to the Planning Process

The broad cross-section of sectors on the consortium helped to encourage linkage between the climate change action plan and individual agency and sector planning processes. Although there is no explicit linkage between the actions envisioned by the climate change action plan and the different individual sector plans, the consortium recognizes that linking the two plans is a necessary part of the process of reducing GHG emissions and has put this linkage as one of its goals. There is a good likelihood that the process will continue to evolve and that the consortium will continue to advocate for its goals. The fact that the consortium continues to meet and be involved in climate change issues lends weight to this likelihood.

3.3.1 Energy Planning

Delaware's SEO is responsible for preparing the state's energy plan. SEO reviews the plan annually and periodically revises it to reflect needs and opportunities in the state. However, according to John Byrne, Director of the Center for Energy and Environmental Policy at the University of Delaware:

---

[19] Source: "State Planning for Greenhouse Gas Mitigation: Transportation and the Delaware Climate Change Action Plan," presented to the ENO Transportation Foundation Seminar Series on Global Climate Change, March 2001.

The action elements of the plan are limited to the governmental, school, and hospital sectors. Delaware's other energy-using sectors (including private and commercial transportation) are encouraged, but not required, to adopt the plans objectives. The creation of a State Energy Task Force by the Governor represents a major effort to upgrade energy planning in Delaware. The SEO and several state agencies (including the Department of Transportation) are active in the Task Forces' work, as are many of the state's leading industries.

Much of the momentum from the climate change action plan has been absorbed into the energy plan effort, and the climate change action plan is serving as a framework for the included transportation, traditional economic supply/demand, and other goals. This effort is intended to involve all the major stakeholders and achieve the same agreement and broad-based vision as the climate change action plan. Considerable linkage between the two plans is envisioned. However, the energy plan is still in its formative stages and was not available for review.

3.3.2 Transportation Planning

Transportation is one of the sectors explicitly considered in Delaware's climate change action plan. As Delaware's most current statewide transportation plan was written before the climate change action plan was issued, it does not reference the plan. However, the statewide transportation plan acknowledges that "travel on Delaware's roads contributes about 24 percent of the total emissions of the two pollutants that make up ozone," and that Delaware exceeds the federal standards for these pollutants. DelDOT is an active member of the consortium and was involved in and agreed with all of the decisions made. The fact that Delaware includes a metropolitan area out of attainment for ozone provides an additional incentive and lever for achieving reductions in VMT. Members are hopeful that future transportation plans will reflect the goals and actions developed by and detailed in the climate change action plan, even though the plan explicitly recognizes that some of these strategies are outside its control.

The consortium conducted an in-depth analysis of the current transportation sector situation and contemplated five categories of policies to reduce the transportation sector's CO_2 emissions:

- Increase CAFE standards for vehicles.
- Provide incentives for the purchase/sale of fuel-efficient vehicles.
- Use statewide mandates and market mechanisms to encourage the adoption and rapid market penetration of AFVs.
- Reduce vehicle miles traveled by adopting policies to implement transportation control measures.
- Develop policies aimed at changing land use patterns.

Within these broad policy categories, the climate change action plan developed three strategies for reducing CO_2 emissions:

- Improve the fuel economy of cars and light-duty trucks.

- Increase the use of alternative fueled vehicles.
- Promote state and local adoption of menus of transportation control measures (TCMs.)

Within each of these strategies, the consortium analyzed the options available for reducing emissions. Accepted options were then evaluated to determine whether they would fit into the "Modest" (10 percent reduction in CO_2 emissions), "Major" (20 percent reduction), or "Full" (36 percent reduction) scenarios. Examples of the actions contemplated within each scenario are shown in Table 5.

Table 5. Delaware: Scenarios to Reduce CO_2 Emissions

- **Fuel Efficiency Improvements**
  - *Modest* – 2 mpg for Passenger Cars and Light Duty Trucks
  - *Major* – 5.9 mpg for Passenger Cars, 3.4 mpg for Light Duty Trucks
  - *Full Implementation* – 7.7 mpg for Passenger Cars, 6.6 mpg for Light Duty Trucks
- **AFVs**
  - *Modest* – 1 percent Compressed Natural Gas (CNG) Fleet Penetration
  - *Major* – 2 percent CNG Fleet Penetration
  - *Full Implementation* – 3.5 percent CNG & 2.5 percent Electric Vehicle Fleet Penetration
- **TCMs**
  - *Modest* – 3 percent Reduction in VMT
  - *Major* – 11 percent Reduction in VMT
  - *Full Implementation* – 20 percent Reduction in VMT

3.4   Results to Date

The actions recommended in the 2000 climate change action plan have not yet been implemented as the momentum for these actions has been absorbed into the effort to develop the energy plan. As a result, no measurable reductions in GHG emissions have been documented to date. However, the consortium's public outreach and education efforts have fostered widespread awareness of these issues.

The consortium recommended the adoption of the "Major Commitment" scenario and its 24 percent reduction in CO_2 emissions. No actions have been implemented, however, as consortium members are waiting to see the results of the energy plan, which will absorb the goals under the "Major commitment" scenario. As the energy plan is being initiated by the governor's office, it should be readily implemented.

Consortium members are optimistic that GHG emission reduction policies and actions will be implemented in Delaware, due in large part to the participation and demonstrated commitment of major corporations like DuPont and other key stakeholder groups in the climate change process. Since DuPont plays a major corporate role in Delaware, it would be difficult to achieve

---

[20] Source: "State Planning for Greenhouse Gas Mitigation: Transportation and the Delaware Climate Change Action Plan," presented by Dr. John Byrne to the ENO Transportation Foundation Seminar Series on Global Climate Change, March 2001.

significant CO_2 reductions without its cooperation. DuPont's cooperation is likely as its representatives have been involved in the climate change planning process from the beginning.

3.5   How the Process Has Evolved

The Delaware process began with its smart growth plans, which involved significant thinking about issues like GHG emissions. However, Delaware's smart growth plans have not yet received widespread support nor produced tangible results.

The Climate Change Consortium considered and used these smart growth efforts and the results of the state's GHG inventory to develop the climate change action plan, which has subsequently been absorbed into ongoing efforts to develop an energy plan. Support and involvement have grown for the recommendations of the climate change action plan and for accomplishment of actions to reduce GHG emissions with each subsequent plan.

3.6   Lessons Learned

Delaware is a small state, which may make its results somewhat atypical. However, there are certain aspects of its process that other interested states could replicate. Some aspects of its process are unique to Delaware but nonetheless worth noting as they contributed to the state's success.

- **Combining smart growth and energy perspectives can broaden participation in the climate change process.** Delaware approached the issue of GHG emissions from both smart growth and energy perspectives. Having both perspectives represented may have promoted greater participation in the climate change process than might have been possible with a foundation in one perspective alone.

- **Broad participation and a consensus-based process are keys to success.** The broad range of stakeholders and consensus-based decision-making process used by the Climate Change Consortium were key to Delaware's progress. The process the consortium used to develop the climate change action plan – namely, smaller issue-based working groups bringing recommendations to the larger consortium and unanimous agreement on all recommendations – is a model that other states and local areas might find valuable.

- **Commitment of participants is needed to cultivate the commitment of agencies.** Individual members of the consortium were committed long term to the issue of GHG reduction. They continue to be advocates for the commitment of their agencies on climate change issues.

- **The private sector plays a vital role.** The participation of the private sector, particularly DuPont, was critical to the action plan. Because DuPont is a major economic factor in Delaware, its participation will likely prove essential to successful implementation of GHG reduction measures.

- **Involving an independent entity broadens the policies and actions considered.** Having the consortium housed in an independent facility may have made it easier for consortium members to consider all actions independent of possible political motive. Members could then consider political realities when contemplating whether agencies would agree to an action.

- **Strong technical analysis demonstrates credibility.** The quality of the technical analysis used to develop forecast models, baselines, scenarios, and cost-effectiveness measures established credibility for the process and contributed to substantive debate on options. As a result, members who were originally skeptical were encouraged to accept the efficacy of the recommended actions and to support the plan.

- **The development of a variety of scenarios improves decision-making.** The consortium developed and considered scenarios with different GHG reduction targets. These scenarios provided consortium members with clear information on the trade-offs and sectoral contributions required to meet the GHG goals and contributed to a high quality of debate.

- **Policies evolve and grow to produce results.** Delaware demonstrates that smart growth, climate change, and energy policies can be complementary and evolve from one policy to another.

4. PORTLAND AND MULTNOMAH COUNTY, OREGON

4.1   Introduction

Portland is a pioneer among U.S. cities in developing climate change action plans. In the early 1990s, it joined an international group of 12 local governments developing climate change solutions as part of the Urban CO_2 Reduction Project coordinated by ICLEI. The local governments set an aggressive goal of reducing CO_2 emissions 20 percent below their 1988 levels. Portland proposed that it attain this goal by 2010 – a 42 percent reduction from the 2010 forecast.[21]

In 1993, Portland became the first U.S. city to adopt a plan to reduce CO_2 emissions. Seven years later, Portland modified its original ambitious goal to reflect rapid population growth. The 2001 "Local Action Plan on Global Warming" (LAP), developed by Portland and Multnomah County, sets a target to reduce CO_2 10 percent below 1990 levels by 2010.[22]

Portland's GHG planning benefited from consistent and strong political leadership from Mayor Vera Katz and Commissioner Erik Sten. The county board of commissioners and the city council have been strong supporters of the LAP and related land use, energy, environmental plans:

---

[21] Source: "Global Warming Strategy," City Council Resolution, November 1993, http://www.sustainableportland.org/GW%20Reduction%20Strategy.pdf.
[22] Source: http://www.sustainableportland.org/Portland%20Global%20Warming%20Plan.pdf.

Portland and cities throughout the world are responsible for creating a sustainable future for our children. We know that cutting emissions is not only smart for the environment, it's great for business, too. If we reduce our CO_2 emissions, we also reduce local air pollution, plant more trees, lower energy bills for residents and business, use more solar and wind power, and create a more liveable, walkable, community-oriented city for all of us. Cities must take a leadership role.

Mayor Vera Katz, "Portland Local Action Plan on Global Warming," 2001

GHG policy and planning play important roles in Portland and complement land use, energy, environmental, and transportation planning. Portland expects its GHG plans to not only reduce GHG emissions, but also improve other aspects of the environment, conserve energy, and make the city more "liveable."

4.2 Approach

In 1993, Portland became the first city in the United States to formally adopt a plan to reduce CO_2 emissions. Multnomah County joined in 2001 and included climate change as a key element of its sustainability program. Portland has taken a comprehensive institutional and technical approach to GHG planning, including developing strong political support through Mayor Katz, Commissioner Sten, the county board of commissioners, and the city council.

4.2.1 Who Is Involved and Why

Portland's GHG planning has benefited from strong and early political leadership on climate change planning and related land use, energy, environmental, and transportation initiatives. These initiatives greatly increase the likelihood that the actions in the LAP will be implemented. The city council unanimously voted to adopt the CO_2 plan, including its dates, related resolutions, and a call for the United States to support international efforts to reduce GHG emissions. In Portland, elected city council members are appointed as commissioners of the city's agencies, providing strong political leadership. Commissioner Sten is responsible for Portland's global warming plan.

Portland is motivated to develop GHG planning for a variety of explicit and subtle reasons. A key incentive is concern over the global and regional impacts of climate change. Regional impacts include:

- Wetter winters and drier summers.
- Reduced Columbia River summer flows by 30 to 50 percent.
- Increased coastal flooding and erosion.
- Decreased forest health and productivity.
- Further decline in the quality of salmon habitat.

In response to stakeholder comments, the LAP concedes that it provides only a preliminary step toward "sustainable GHG emissions" based on IPCC estimates that reductions of 60-70 percent below 1990 levels will be necessary to stabilize GHG concentrations. The LAP notes that, "While the actions of any single municipality can impact only a small fraction of emissions, collaboration of a large number of urban areas can achieve meaningful reductions."

According to local contacts, there are three additional incentives for GHG planning in Portland:

- Reducing emissions leads to an attractive, liveable, and economically vibrant community. Actions to implement the LAP not only contribute to reducing climate change but also to developing desirable aspects of living identified by the community.
- Contributing to reducing climate change impacts provides Portland with a sense of "stewardship."
- Understanding the sources of regional emissions and the technical and institutional feasibility of options to reduce these emissions early will better prepare Portland to take future actions.

Finally, Portland may see an additional benefit in developing the LAP. By addressing global climate change, Portland may be able to offer a business environment that reflects adjustments for climate change action – the same type of business environment that will increasingly be encountered within the European Union and other countries ratifying the Kyoto Protocol.

The 2001 LAP was developed through collaboration with and input from the public, businesses, utilities, the private sector, non-profit organizations, and city and county agencies. However, on-going GHG planning does not involve standing committees like the consortium that developed the Delaware GHG plan, or formal commitments like the New Jersey Covenants. Instead, partnerships are formed, sometimes with incentives, to undertake specific projects. For example, the green building program offered financial incentives up to $20,000 to major construction projects that met the LEED™ green building standard and improved energy efficiency at least 20 percent beyond code.

4.2.2 Climate Change Action Plan

The 2001 LAP sets a goal of a 10 percent emissions reduction below 1990 levels by 2010. The most recent update to the plan also assesses progress and emphasizes education.[23]

As part of the planning process, Portland developed comprehensive baseline GHG inventories using electric and gas utilities data, state agency data on transportation fuel use data, EIA data on fossil fuel consumption, and city data on waste collection. The baseline analysis generally used the methodology provided by ICLEI, with a major modification for emissions from electricity.

The detailed baseline information in the LAP is for Multnomah County GHG emissions in metric tons of CO_2 equivalent total per capita by sector. The major categories in Table 6 are sub-divided by fuel source, provided historically for 1990, 1995, 1999, and forecast for 2010.

---

[23] Source: Susan Anderson, Director of the Office of Sustainable Development.

40

Table 6. Per Capita Multnomah County GHG Emissions by Sector (Million Metric Tons)[24]

	1990	1995	1999	2010 Forecast
Residential	3.43	2.91	2.99	3.15
Commercial	3.15	3.29	3.45	3.70
Industrial	2.69	2.79	2.79	3.10
Transportation	6.36	6.26	6.25	7.51
Solid Waste	1.37	0.92	0.98	0.07*

* Expected to fall as a result of EPA regulations requiring landfills to capture methane.

Total GHG emissions in Multnomah County increased from 9.9 million metric tons in 1990 to 10.6 million metric tons in 1999. By 2010, emissions are forecast to increase over 20 percent from 1990 levels to 12.0 million metric tons. The 10 percent reduction goal will require at total reduction of 26 percent, or 3.1 million metric tons. Table 7 shows how the LAP divides this reduction goal into five primary components.

Table 7. GHG Reduction Targets (Million Metric Tons), Portland and Multnomah County

Target	Emissions Reductions
Transportation, Telecommunications, and Access	1.35
Energy Efficiency	0.67
Renewable Resources	0.54
Solid Waste Management	0.23
Forestry and Carbon Offsets	0.31
Total	**3.10**

The sixth component, "Policy, Research, and Education," is designed to "enhance the success" of the other components.

Each component includes objectives, which have either a "government activity" primarily affecting Portland or Multnomah County's own operations or a "community initiative" that can include local government and community partner involvement. It is important to note that some strategies are outside the responsibility of Portland. These activities are targeted for completion by either 2003 or 2010.

The "Transportation, Telecommunications, and Access" component is assigned the largest share of reductions. The LAP observes that in 1990 transportation accounted for 37 percent of local GHG emissions, grew to 38 percent in 1999, and is forecast to grow to 43 percent by 2010. The LAP includes transportation actions that involve federal, state, and local actions. The major strategies to reduce GHG emissions in this component are to reduce VMT and improve fuel economy.

The LAP identifies the following "Principles for Reducing Transportation Emissions:"

---

[24] Source: "Local Action Plan for Global Warming," 2001.

- Reduce the need for trips by using telecommunications.
- Encourage travel by foot, bicycle, transit, or ridesharing.
- Implement mechanisms to ensure that drivers pay the full social cost of driving.
- Improve access to alternative fuel and highly fuel-efficient vehicles.

The actions support the framework of TEA-21, implementation of the state transportation planning rule to coordinate land use and transportation planning, "state benchmarks for land use, air quality, mobility, and global warming," and implementation of the State Transportation Plan. Government transportation actions and community transportation initiatives are detailed in Tables 8 and 9.

Table 8. Government Transportation Actions, Portland and Multnomah County

By 2003	By 2010
• Require city and county agencies to offer bus tickets to visitors as an alternative to driving and parking. • Implement policies to encourage transit for city and county business travel.	• Reduce employee VMT in city and county vehicles by 20 percent by promoting teleconferencing and the availability of pedestrian, bicycle, transit, and rideshare options. • Promote telework and flexible hours to enable 25 percent of employees to use these options.

Table 9. Community Transportation Initiatives, Portland and Multnomah County

By 2003	By 2010
• Support expanded transit on major transit arterials. • Work with the Portland area transit authority, Tri-Met, to improve access to transit. • Work with businesses to offer "cash out" or equivalent payment for those employees who do use subsidized parking. • Promote growth through redevelopment and infill that encourages living near workplaces.	• Provide transit passes to all residents funded through a household levy or business tax. • Continue signal optimisation plans for vehicles, bicycles, and cyclists. • Promote telework and other flexible-schedule work options. • Promote vehicle sharing. • Expand education in schools to promote safe alternatives to single-occupancy cars. • Support the use of auto insurance premiums based on miles cars are driven. • Support congestion pricing on appropriate regional roadways. • Advocate raising federal CAFE standards for new automobiles to 45 mpg. • Promote efficient options such as high-speed rail between Northwest urban centers.

Evaluation of progress is an innovative aspect of the LAP. Actions are monitored by inventorying GHG emissions annually. Every two years, Portland provides a report on progress that includes critical information for updating and refining the plan. "Global Warming Updates" on progress are issued periodically. Evaluation promotes transparency and accountability of the planning process and establishes credibility, which is important for continuity and future expansion of efforts.

4.3   Links to the Planning Process

There is a broad range of state, regional, and local regulations, plans, and initiatives that provide support and a frame of reference for local GHG planning. The LAP benefits from its ability to demonstrate that its actions support and implement state comprehensive planning goals, that it is endorsed in the state GHG plan, and that it supports the integrated approach to land use and transportation provided for in the Urban Growth Boundary, the Regional Transportation Plan (RTP), and the Portland Transportation Systems Plan, as described in the next section.

The broad range of planning activities described below provide a context and frame of reference for the LAP. These activities support the LAP even when they do not directly reference climate change and though they do not make Portland's GHG planning inevitable. The community itself appears to provide strong direct support for GHG planning.

Comprehensive planning in Oregon provides broad state goals for planning and standards for all cities and counties to meet. Several of the state planning goals support the goals of the LAP and provide underpinnings for the regional and city transportation and land use plans closely connected to the LAP. The Urban Growth Boundary is designed to encourage compact future growth in order to reduce sprawl and traffic congestion through maximum use of public transit, walking, and bicycling.

The Oregon GHG Plan, produced by the Oregon Office of Energy (OOE) notes that:

> While Oregon has programs for energy efficiency, renewable energy, integrated energy planning, and land use and transportation planning, the state still faces a 32 percent increase in CO_2 emissions between 1990 and 2015. Transportation CO_2 emissions will rise by 44 percent.[25]

The Oregon Progress Board set 259 benchmarks for state policy in its 1994 report to the legislature, including one to hold CO_2 emissions to 1990 levels. When the OOE began GHG planning it recognized that it would take ambitious programs to meet this goal. After completing the inventory and forecast, OOE concluded that "it will take significantly stronger actions...both at the state and federal levels."

---

[25] Source: http://www.energy.state.or.us/climate/gggas htm.

It is noteworthy that the Oregon GHG plan recognizes that it must include federal actions to meet its goals and that many actions are closely linked to transportation, land use, energy, and environmental planning by other state and local agencies.

The Oregon GHG Plan calculates baseline CO_2 emissions attributable to transportation, electric utilities, and natural gas sources for 1990 through 2015. The plan develops the following long-term strategies (Table 10):

Table 10. Long-term Strategies of Oregon GHG Plan

Strategy	Components
Energy efficiency and renewable resources	• Developing cost-effective strategies conserving renewable resources that include costs for CO_2 emissions.
Transportation efficiency	• Increasing the efficiency of the state transportation system to reduce reliance on oil, thereby decreasing pollution, congestion, GHG, and other costs associated with vehicle travel. • Exploring voluntary and market-based incentives for purchasing efficient vehicles. • Promoting the efficient operation of vehicles.
Offsets	• Planting trees to sequester carbon. • Developing other means to increase energy efficiency.
Economic development	• Targeting new technologies for economic development that will contribute the most to furthering state, national, and international climate change goals.
Adaptation to climate change	• Supporting research on the effects of climate change on water, fisheries, agricultural and forestry resources and on sea level rise on the Oregon coast.
Recycle, reuse, and solid waste management	• Reduce the generation of waste. • Recycling and reusing materials.

The Oregon GHG Plan identifies 18 actions to take over the next 5 years, focusing on:

Transportation

- Implement the Oregon Transportation Plan.
- Achieve the goals of the Oregon Transportation Planning Rule.
- Study the potential for encouraging the purchase of efficient vehicles through market-based incentives.
- Inform Oregonians about how to save fuel by adjusting how they operate their vehicles.

> **Goals of the Portland Comprehensive Plan**
>
> - Guide future development.
> - Reduce reliance on automobiles and decrease VMT.
> - Promote public transit to and from central city, regional, and town centers.
> - Encourage mixed-use centers served by a multimodal transportation system.
> - Emphasize infill and redevelopment, transit-oriented development, and links between housing and employment.

<u>Local Government</u>

- Help Portland achieve the goals of its CO_2 Reduction Strategy.

The Portland Comprehensive Plan was adopted in 1980 to meet state requirements for comprehensive planning. State requirements set planning goals, many of which support the Portland LAP and regional and city transportation plans. The comprehensive plan includes goals and policies to guide future development and is amended periodically to reflect changing circumstances.[26] Although the comprehensive plan predates the LAP and does not explicitly mention climate change, it sets a useful context for the LAP. Many of the actions in the LAP, particularly those involving land use and public transit, have a foundation in the comprehensive plan. When the energy element of the comprehensive plan is updated, it will likely include references to GHG emissions and climate change and incorporate many LAP initiatives.

The Climate Trust is a non-profit organization formed in 1997 following passage of an Oregon law requiring new energy facilities to "avoid, sequester, or displace a portion of their previously unregulated CO_2 emissions."[27] The Climate Trust initiates, encourages, and funds projects to reduce GHG emissions and provides outreach and education on actions to prevent climate change. The organization's first priority is to implement CO_2 offset projects for power plants, and its initial activities included grants for innovative projects to reduce CO_2 emissions and a partnership with the OOE to organize community forums on climate change. Funding primarily comes when new power plants are built in Oregon, but the organization may receive funding from other sources. The Climate Trust receives applications for offset projects from within and outside Oregon and has made grants for international projects, such as the forest preservation project in Ecuador.

As mentioned in the Seattle case study, Seattle City Light (SCL), the Seattle electric utility, is an active participant in climate change initiatives. SCL has set a very ambitious goal of no net GHG emissions generated from the power it supplies. Recently, SCL contracted with the Climate Trust for assistance in selecting and acquiring offset projects.

As part of its GHG planning, Portland has received two grants from the Climate Trust. Portland will use the first grant to develop an intelligent transportation systems signal prioritization project, forecast to reduce 148,000 metric tons of carbon equivalent, and a web-based rideshare matching program to simplify and expand area-wide ride-sharing (www.carpoolmatchnw.org). Portland will use the second grant to optimize the timing of traffic signals on local arterials. The Climate Trust is giving Portland these grants in exchange for the resulting CO_2 offsets.

The Climate Trust is relatively young and has not yet produced significant GHG emissions reductions. However, the organization appears to have great potential. Its innovative aspects include:

---

[26] Source: http://www.planning.ci.portland.or.us/pdf/ComprehensivePlan.pdf.
[27] Source: http://www.climatetrust.org/.

- **Partnerships**. The Climate Trust partners with utilities, public agencies conducting GHG planning, and project initiators. The Climate Trust not only funds projects throughout the state, but also conducts education with funding from utilities and other sources.

- **Flexible project eligibility**. The Climate Trust works with applicants from Oregon, other states, and other countries.

- **Rigorous project selection and monitoring.** The Climate Trust selects and monitors projects to assure that they result in net GHG emissions reductions. Using monitoring and verification plans, the Climate Trust works to prevent the "leakage" of benefits. In addition, the organization uses surveys, trip diaries, and other means to evaluate reductions from baselines.

4.3.1 Energy Planning

The Oregon and Portland energy offices play lead roles in their respective climate change plans. The Portland Office of Sustainable Development has shared responsibility for energy policy and the LAP, ensuring close coordination between climate change and energy planning. As noted, the OOE is the lead agency for the state GHG plan. Many of the other case study areas have similar connections to energy planning. The broad commitment of Portland, the region, and the state to integrated environmental, land use, transportation, and smart growth planning provides the LAP with a broad foundation.

4.3.2 Transportation Planning

The Portland Office of Transportation, a separate agency within the city government, participated in developing the LAP and is responsible for the Transportation System Plan (TSP).[28] The TSP has numerous substantial links to the LAP, including:

- Supporting the Region's 2040 Growth Concept, which calls for "maintaining thriving communities and a healthy economy while containing urban sprawl."
- Encouraging a broad range of attractive transportation choices.
- Promoting the environmental sustainability of transportation, including explicit identification of the impacts of transportation on GHG levels.

Metro, the federally designated MPO for the Portland metropolitan area, develops the RTP. Among other regional goals, the RTP seeks to coordinate land use and transportation planning to reduce VMT. The RTP is closely linked to other state, regional, and local transportation, land use, and transportation planning initiatives. As such, it too provides a supportive foundation for the LAP through consistent policies and initiatives. However, the RTP does not appear to explicitly include the reduction of GHG emissions as a goal alongside other transportation, land use, and environmental goals.

---

[28] Source: http://www.trans.ci.portland.or.us/Planning/TSPSummary.htm#Draft.

4.4   Results to Date

Results in GHG emissions in Portland and Multnomah County have been mixed, with local reductions tempered by population growth and associated increases in energy use and miles traveled. According to the April 2002 update,

- Per capita emissions of local CO_2 decreased 2 percent from 2000 to 2001 and were more than 7 percent below 1990 levels in 2001. For comparison, national per capita emissions have increased 0.7 percent over the same period. (Portland planners credit the per capita decreases to the success of the electricity conservation efforts of utilities, the state of Oregon, and Portland.)
- From 1990 to 1999, total local CO_2 emissions grew each year, rising at an annual rate of 0.7 percent.
- Between 1990 and 2001, total CO_2 emissions in Multnomah County increased from 9.9 million to 10.4 million metric tons, a rise of just over 6 percent.
- While Portland is one of only a few places reducing overall emissions, it still is only a small step towards the city's goal of an absolute reduction to 10 percent below 1990 levels by 2010.[29]

The 2001 LAP provides a broad array of actions to accomplish this ambitious goal. In the future, evaluations should indicate both quantitatively and qualitatively the success of the elements of the plan.

4.5   How the Process Has Evolved

GHG policy and planning play important roles in Portland and complement land use, energy, environmental, and transportation planning. In fact, Portland's approach is different from many other cities' approaches, where GHG goals can be secondary outgrowths of energy, smart growth, or air quality plans. For example, many other cities estimate the GHG emissions reductions of decisions that have already been made, indicating that decisions to expand public transit or ride-sharing, which are made primarily for traditional transportation reasons, also reduce CO_2 emissions by shifting demand away from automobile travel. In contrast, GHG planning in Portland has relatively high visibility. Participants in the process expect climate change planning and the LAP to contribute to advancing climate change goals, improving other aspects of the environment, and making the area move "liveable."

4.6   Lessons Learned

Portland provides a very useful model for other areas considering initiating or expanding climate change planning. The city has been a pioneer among U.S. cities, having been active in this policy area since the early 1990s. In 1993, Portland became the first U.S. city to formally adopt a GHG plan. Portland's progress is due in large part to its political leadership and long-standing tradition of integrated state, regional, and local energy, environmental, land use, and transportation planning. Political leadership and linked planning provide a supportive planning

---

[29] Source: http://www.sustainableportland.org/engery_global_warming_2001_emissions.pdf

context for the LAP. For example, LAP actions that encourage infill, transportation alternatives, and public transit can be firmly connected to state, regional, and local regulations, policies, and plans.

This research identified several key lessons learned:

- **Political champions play an important role.** Political champions play a critical role in climate change planning in Portland and have been critical to the success of the LAP.

- **International activities and support can provide useful information.** Portland was an early participant in the ICLEI coordinated initiatives of international cities to reduce climate change. Portland benefited from the information exchange and mutual support of its international peers and from the technical tools provided through ICLEI.

- **A broad planning context can foster progress.** The Portland climate change planning process demonstrates that state, regional, and local regulations, policies and plans can contribute to climate change planning by encouraging the integration of energy, environmental, land use, and transportation planning.

- **Partnerships can provide innovative solutions.** The Climate Trust is an innovative initiative involving partnerships between non-profit organizations, utilities seeking offset credits, and a broad range of project initiators, including Portland. The Climate Trust provides outreach and education, receives funds from utilities and other sources, and applies an innovative technical process to select projects and monitor results.

- **Evaluating progress is critical.** Evaluating progress is an important aspect of climate change planning in Portland. LAP actions are monitored annually by inventorying GHG emissions. Every two years, a report evaluates progress, provides information for updating the plan, and identifies new issues. Evaluation promotes the transparency and accountability of the climate change planning process and establishes the credibility needed to continue progress already made.

- **Opportunities to expand links can encourage further progress.** Portland has made impressive progress in promoting comprehensive and continuous climate change planning. Tri-Met (the regional transportation agency) and Metro (the regional MPO) plan and implement land use and transportation initiatives that strongly support climate change goals, although this support does not appear to be explicit. Other opportunities to further elevate support for climate change may exist by considering climate change planning alongside transportation goals in the planning process.

5. SEATTLE AND KING COUNTY, WASHINGTON

5.1   Introduction

King County, Washington, and its largest city, Seattle, are linked by geography and a shared concern about taking local action to reduce GHG emissions produced in their overlapping jurisdictions. Both are developing, implementing, and monitoring GHG action plans. Although these plans are being produced through separate political processes, each plan's success is dependent on the other's success. There is a broad range of planning and policy work underway in the city and county related to climate change, although GHG plans were not complete at the time of this research.

Seattle and King County also have a great deal of activity underway related to smart growth and energy planning, with rapidly evolving links to GHG reduction. King County Council Member Cynthia Sullivan summarized this critical interrelationship during a regional meeting in January 2002:

> This campaign is a reminder that the effort to reduce air pollution has no borders, and that everyone must get involved. Individuals and communities have made great strides in reducing GHG emissions. It's time for government to work with those communities and each other in developing programs that ease air pollution, because it is both an environmental and public health problem.

Seattle identified climate change as a local concern in the early 1990s. The city links clean air and climate change issues, pursuing strategies that reduce both air pollution and GHG emissions. Seattle established the Office of Sustainability and the Environment to deal with these linkages and other related concerns.

Climate change work to date has focused on significant expected regional impacts. Local reports predict that rising temperatures in the Pacific Northwest will cause wetter winters and drier summers, reduce river flows, increase coastal flooding and erosion, and decrease forest health and productivity. The region is especially concerned about preserving snow pack, which is a natural storage system for water supply and hydroelectricity. The snow pack is predicted to decrease by half within the next generation.

The Office of Sustainability and Environment focuses on complex challenges such as air quality, conserving water and energy in city facilities, sustainable building, and chemical use reduction. The office recognizes that responding to these challenges not only will improve quality of life in the community, but also will address climate change concerns. As former Mayor Paul Schell said in 2001:

> Every city and every individual can take steps to reduce global warming. Cities are where most emissions occur – and where the solutions must begin. We can't afford to wait for the federal government to do this.

Early in 2002, King County Executive Ron Sims signed an Executive Order that directed all county offices to pursue a Clean Air Initiative. This initiative established an executive policy to reduce emissions of GHG and other significant air pollutants from all county operations and to develop programs and policies that encourage reductions from all sources in the region. This policy was the result of an organized effort that Executive Sims and the council initiated in May 2001 when Seattle hosted the symposium "Climate Change and the Pacific Northwest: What Can and Should Local Government Do." Executive Sims described why King County is involved in climate change:

> As local governments, we feel the consequences of climate change – for water supply, salmon recovery, flood control, and energy. We also control many important factors affecting climate change – from land use, transportation, building standards, and waste disposal. As elected leaders, it would be irresponsible not to prepare our communities for the future; we need to do more.

5.2   Seattle's Approach

The city of Seattle is also developing a strategic climate change action plan to assist in reducing GHG emissions. Seattle's focus has evolved and expanded from energy conservation to air pollution to climate change. In comparison, King County has historically focused on managing land development and natural resources. Both Seattle and King County governments address transportation, construction codes, smart growth, and energy conservation. The state developed a GHG mitigation plan in 1996, which appears to be more of a resource for the Seattle and King County plans than a critical source of direction.

Seattle has been interested in energy conservation since 1977, when it decided to pursue energy conservation rather then investing in nuclear power. In the early stages of developing its energy policy, the city concentrated on education and on improving construction methods in the industrial, commercial, and residential sectors. The city established financial incentives in the form of grants, rebates, and low interest loans, and also pursued stricter regulations on energy efficiency in construction.

In 1994, the Neighborhood Power Project (NPP) was introduced as part of a city energy conservation project. Under the direction of SCL, the city-owned power company, the NPP was a community-based initiative to improve the efficiency of energy use in the city and to promote conservation in neighborhoods. SCL, one of the largest utilities in the United States, became a "Climate Wise" partner with the EPA in 1997. As a Climate Wise partner, the utility company helped form relationships with businesses to reduce GHG emissions based on four key objectives:

- Establish a process to identify and implement energy efficiency, waste reduction methods, and other measures that meet business needs and reduce GHG emissions.
- Work with business partners to help them submit to SCL and EPA a customized Climate Wise Action Plan identifying steps to achieve the first objective.
- Review and update the plan as needed and strive for continuous improvement.

- Track, report, and inform all the stakeholders and the public about the activities.

In 2001, Seattle took over the Climate Wise program from SCL and began formulating a long-range plan to deal with GHG emissions. The mayor and city council strongly supported these actions.

In July 2001, the city passed Resolution 30316, which supports the Kyoto Protocol and calls on other local governments to do the same. Through this resolution, Seattle expressed the hope that it would adopt the goal of reducing GHG emissions by 7 percent from 1990 baseline levels by 2010. To help meet this goal, the city first needs to perform a GHG emissions inventory. Resolution 30316 also formalizes SCL's commitment to becoming the first major utility in the country to achieve zero net GHG emissions. SCL will meet this goal by eliminating plants that have high GHG emissions, mitigating emissions, using renewable energy, and promoting energy efficiency and conservation.

5.3   King County's Approach

In 1998, King County introduced a Smart Growth Initiative to address growth management and sprawl. Comments by Executive Sims appear to indicate that he supports the methods outlined in the Smart Growth Initiative to address regional growth comprehensively and to attempt to encourage a balance for the community through an improved transportation system, adequate housing, promotion of liveable communities, and protection of environmental resources. The county's transit agency, Metro Transit, became a partner with the SCL Climate Wise Program in 2000. The two made a concerted effort to work together on growth-related issues.

In 2001, the county participated in a symposium that focused on how local governments can work together to combat climate change. During the symposium, the county identified several steps it was undertaking to address climate change, including:

- Reducing the use of fresh water and increasing the use of reclaimed water to deal with the water shortages that could result from climate change.
- Incorporating climate change into flood control and waste water infrastructure planning.
- Converting vehicles to gas-electric hybrids as the county fleet is replaced.
- Developing methane gas emissions projects in landfills and wastewater facilities.
- Promoting extensive recycling programs.
- Promoting commute trip reduction programs.
- Working with Seattle and suburban governments to expand the Smart Growth Initiative.
- Using bio-solids from treatment plants as fertilizer for forests and farms.
- Inventorying emissions from all county operations.

These steps are part of the county's Earth Legacy Initiatives, a program to address climate change. The Earth Legacy Initiatives program was later supplemented with the Clean Air Initiative, which made GHG reduction a county policy for all departments.

In early 2002, the county council unanimously approved a motion supporting participation in the CCPC created by ICLEI. The CCPC emerged from an international summit held at United Nations headquarters to slow GHG emissions around the world. Participants in the CCPC receive technical advice, including applications of models and data collection to define baseline GHG emissions, contact with other communities involved in the program, and limited financial support. King County joined several other participants from the Pacific Northwest, including Seattle, Portland, and Vancouver. As part of the CPP campaign, King County is working on an emissions inventory and climate change action plan.

5.4   Who is Involved and Why

There are several key people and agencies representing government, business, and nonprofit groups involved in regional climate change efforts. Within Seattle, former Mayor Schell and several city council members provided initial leadership. An office in SCL provided initial leadership on environmental and energy policies. Leadership was subsequently provided through the Seattle Office of Sustainability and the Environment.

Executive Sims provided the leadership for climate change in the county alongside political support from the council. The DNR provided direction on programs, including developing an emissions inventory and educational materials and providing support to the Air Quality Steering Team (AQST). The AQST is responsible for the overall direction of air quality initiatives, including researching, developing, and monitoring plans and providing educational materials. The executive cabinet reviews documents and plans from the executive office and the AQST.

Many businesses, schools, non-profit groups, and government agencies voluntarily participate in the SCL Climate Wise Program. Seattle's public schools, Seattle University, Boeing, Pepsi, and King County Metro Transit are examples of public and private participants in the energy conservation programs sponsored by the SCL Climate Wise Program. Two active non-profit groups that have partnered with SCL are The Climate Neutral Network and the Climate Trust. Both partnerships involve emissions trading, financial aid to businesses to support participation, and technical advice on ways program participants can conserve energy.

5.5   Links to the Planning Process

The planning processes for both the city and county are in the development stages. With the help of CCPC, both are developing climate change action plans. Once developed, these plans will detail and formalize the current emissions inventories and define goals, policies, implementation processes, and methods to monitor and update the overall process. Until last year, policies and programs related to GHG emissions and climate change had been developed on a somewhat ad hoc basis; most efforts involved voluntary commitments from various public and private entities.

As indicated in Figure 6, the EPA helped SCL begin operating local initiatives through the Climate Wise Program by providing funds and technical advice. These efforts focused on energy conservation, recycling, and commute trip reduction programs. On a voluntary basis, actions were incorporated into each business, government agency, or school's Climate Wise Action Plan. These actions were not part of a coordinated citywide planning process, but rather were incremental initial efforts that achieved numerous small successes with minimal investment. The new Office for Sustainability and the Environment took over this program in 2002, resulting in a more concerted effort to plan actions that can be implemented through either SCL or the DNR. The county planning process has been focused on smart growth policies, transportation planning, and resource planning. Both city and county strategies will continue to evolve as they promote climate change policies that complement other policy concerns, particularly air quality and quality of life.

This review indicates that Seattle and King County share concerns about climate change and regularly discuss their action plans. In addition, both are employing some of the same strategies to reduce GHG emissions. For example, both are members of ICLEI's CCPC and jointly hosted a symposium on how local governments can approach climate change issues. Some common policies include employing building codes that improve energy efficiency and promoting the Trip Reduction Program. County Executive Sims stated that he would like to work with Seattle and suburban communities on growth management plans to preserve and protect regional natural resources and on efforts to better manage the generation of GHG emissions.

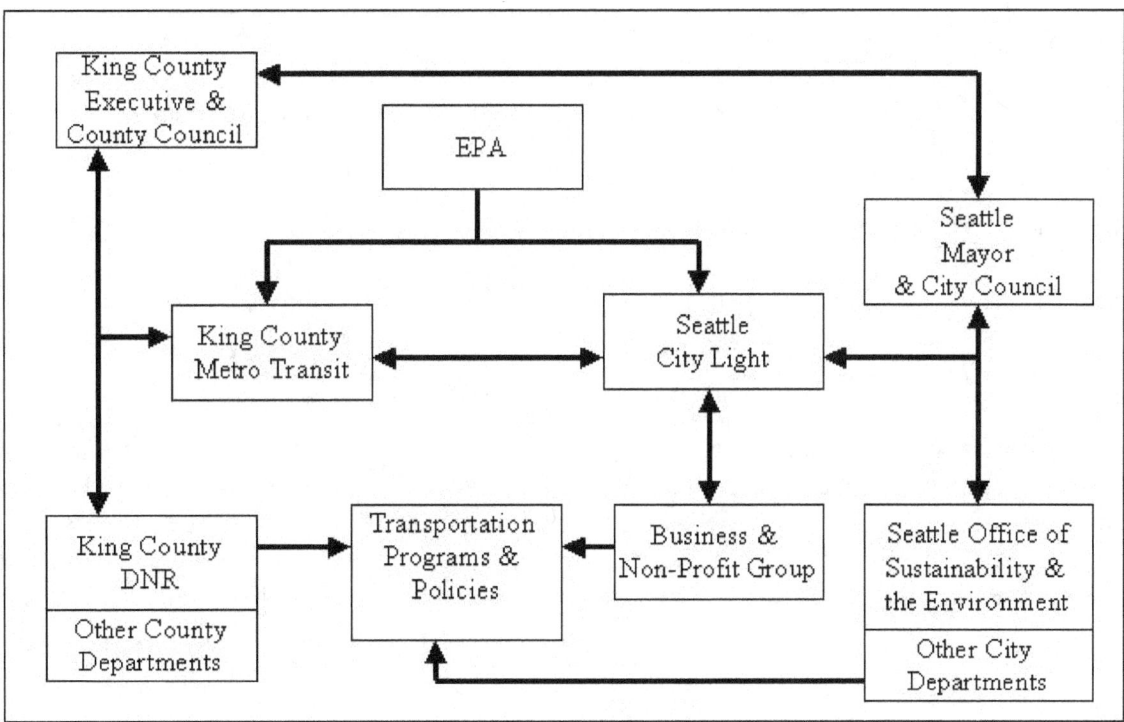

Figure 6. Climate Change Planning Process for King County Region, Washington State[30]

---

[30] Source: USDOT/Volpe Center, 2002.

5.5.1 Energy Planning

Seattle and King County are involved in active energy planning. An April 2000 symposium on energy planning in Seattle focused on developing an outline for the region's clean energy action plan. Over 200 people from government, business, the media, and non-profit groups attended. The resulting plan identified public and private sector actions that position the Pacific Northwest and British Columbia in a leadership role in the global energy transformation. Participants expect that successful implementation of these actions will reduce GHG emissions regionally.

The action plan identified seven key objectives:

- **Economic Development.** Promote economic development and trade initiatives to build a clean energy industry.

- **Energy Efficiency.** Meet half of the region's new demand for heat, light, and power through increased energy efficiency.

- **Renewable Resources.** Build a base of renewable energy that can support new self-sustaining markets.

- **Transportation.** Reduce the amount of oil consumed in transportation industry.

- **Environmental Consequences.** Consider environmental costs and consequences in decision-making.

- **GHG.** Reduce GHG emissions and other pollutants.

- **Education.** Teach sustainable development and clean energy practices at all levels.

5.5.2 Transportation Planning

The city and county acknowledge the importance of transportation planning in reducing GHG emissions. Both have developed several similar policies that address energy use within the transportation sector while improving the transportation system itself. Many of these strategies are designed to reduce automobile use and promote public transit or car pools. Figure 7 shows the trends in CO_2 emissions due to fossil fuels in the Washington state transportation industry.

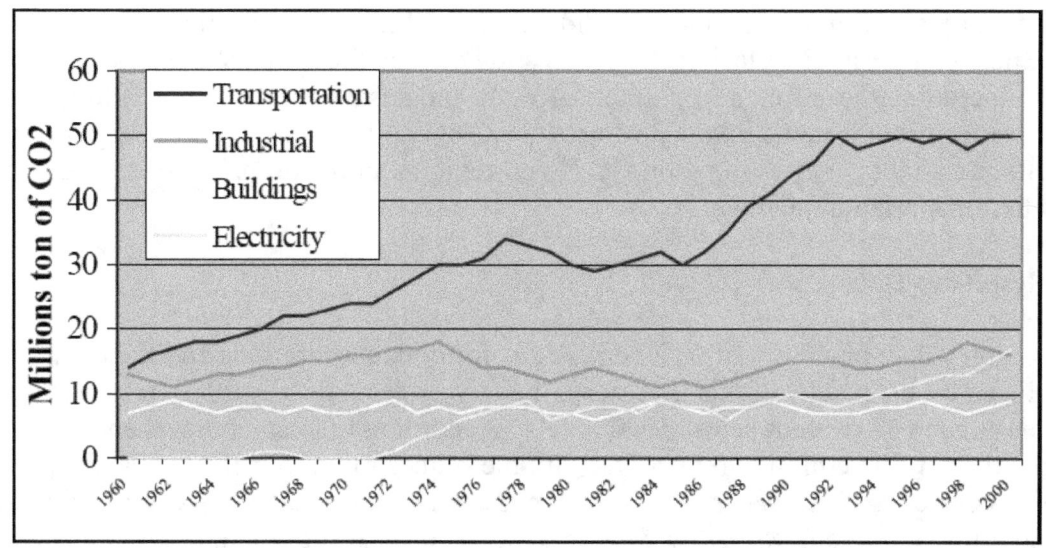

Figure 7. CO$_2$ Emissions from Fossil Fuel Consumption for Washington State[31]

The following lists identify several of the transportation programs and policies Seattle and King County use in their planning process to reduce GHG emissions.

Seattle

- Convert the entire diesel fleet to ultra low sulfur diesel fuel by the end of 2004.
- Purchase additional AFVs as part of a Green Fleet program.
- Monitor smog and notify the public when it is unhealthy for travel, potentially discouraging vehicular traffic.
- Promote the Trip Rate Reduction Project used by several participants in the SCL Climate Wise program to reduce vehicle trips through car pooling or public transit.
- Limit urban sprawl to reduce congestion and provide more efficient transportation.

King County

- Promote the Trip Rate Reduction Project used by several participants of the SCL Climate Wise program to reduce vehicle trips through carpooling or public transit.
- Provide employees with an Area FlexPass, giving them unlimited access to public transit.
- Promote carpooling through discounted parking and priority spaces for multiple occupant vehicles.
- Promote bicycling.
- Promote smart growth and transit-oriented development to discourage automotive trips.

The transportation planning process, as well as the actions of public and private transportation providers in Seattle and King County, will be important elements of any climate change action plans developed. Processes and plans will likely continue to evolve as further linkages are

---

[31] Source: Energy Information Administration Data, Washington State - Adapted by USDOT/Volpe Center.

developed. City and County agencies envision additional linkages within city or county agencies, between the action plans themselves, and between these plans and other planning processes, including those for energy, smart growth, and sustainability. In the future, an increasing priority for establishing goals to reduce GHG emissions may encourage groups like the Puget Sound MPO, the Washington DOT, and regional public transit agencies to expand linkages to transportation planning.

5.6   Results to Date

Seattle completed an inventory of GHG emissions for both corporations and the community as a whole. Based on the results of this inventory, the city projects that by 2010, it will cut corporate GHG emissions to 84 percent below 1990 levels. According to local contacts and reports, combining these GHG emission reductions with the sequestration benefits of banning logging in the 85,000 acres of forested watershed land owned by the city and the emissions reduction from mitigating utility emissions will allow Seattle to achieve large additional reductions in overall GHG emissions. [32]

However, by 2010 community GHG emissions (i.e., emissions within city boundaries) are projected to grow nearly 20 percent over 1990 levels, primarily due to increased emissions from the transportation sector. According to local contacts, to develop a plan to curb the growth in emissions, Seattle is joining a four-county initiative (including King County) led by the Puget Sound Clean Air Agency. In 2003, the agency will launch a stakeholder process to develop a target and plan for GHG emissions that will be supported by citizens, government, and business.

The largest source of GHG emission reductions for Seattle has been the elimination of a coal fire-powered plant. By eliminating this plant, Seattle anticipates reducing over 600,000 metric tons of GHG per year. According to local sources, conservation from the energy sector saved over $114 million in power costs and produced a reduction of nearly 250,000 metric tons of CO_2, equivalent to removing 46,000 cars from the road system.

On the transportation side, the goal of the Commute Rate Reduction Program is to reduce the number and length of all new trips by 35 percent by 2005. As presented in Table 11, the program is also expected to reduce the amount of work trips made in single occupant vehicles by 20 percent by 2010, which is equivalent to removing 20,000 cars from the road every morning. As a result, delays would be reduced by 6 percent as people switch to alternate modes. Investment in the program has increased from the state investment of $2 million in 1995 to over $35 million in business investments in 2000.

---

[32] "Inventory and Report: Seattle's Greenhouse Gas Emissions," City of Seattle, September 2002
http://www.cityofseattle net/environment/Documents/GHG_Report.pdf

Table 11. Travel Modes for Work Trips, Seattle[33]

Mode of Transportation	Base 1990	Goal	
		2000	2010
Single Occupant Car	59%	51%	35%
Non-Single Occupant Car			
Carpool	12%	12%	13%
Public Transit	16%	20%	27%
Bicycle	3%	5%	9%
Walk	7%	8%	10%
Work at home	3%	4%	6%
Total	1.00	1.00	1.00

The conversion of the city's bus fleet to low emission sulfur fuel and AFVs by 2004 is expected to cut toxic emissions by 90 percent.

These are just a few examples of programs implemented by Seattle and King County. City and county government officials believe that once action plans are in place and programs that can be implemented and monitored over time are defined, GHG emissions should be reduced further.[34]

5.7 How the Process Has Evolved

Historically, the region has been concerned with energy and conservation. Seattle has an expanded range of options available because it owns the local utility company. Over time, concern for energy and conservation evolved and expanded to include air quality and, more recently, GHG emissions. As climate change concerns became established in Seattle, outreach efforts and education attracted the interest of businesses, non-profit agencies, and state and local governments. The city and county have benefited from funds and technical support supplied by the EPA and from technical assistance and information sharing among communities working on GHG reduction under the ICLEI's CCPC.

As Seattle and King County develop their climate change action plans, they are defining roles, responsibilities, goals, actions, and processes for implementing actions. Through the continued monitoring of results, Seattle and King County will be able to update and adjust planning to ensure maximum progress and foster political support.

5.8 Lessons Learned

Seattle and King County are building on the historic relationships they have established to solve common problems. Former Seattle Mayor Schell and King County Executive Sims were the initial champions of climate change, along with support from their respective councils. Education and outreach efforts provided a foundation of political and financial support that grew

---

[33] Source: Seattle's Comprehensive Plan.
[34] Source: Press releases by Seattle and King County.

with time. The ability of public agencies, businesses, and citizens in the area to continue to link energy, environment, and transportation decisions will determine the success of both the city and the county climate change action plans.

This research identified several lessons learned:

- **The evolution of policy from energy to air quality to climate change issues is useful.** Seattle and King County provide useful models of how local public policy can evolve from energy concerns to air quality concerns to climate change concerns. This incremental approach takes time, demonstrated progress, and increasing political and public awareness of the complementary linkages among these concerns.

- **Political champions can help start and continue progress.** Although executive leadership by mayors or county executives can be critical to establishing initial momentum, support from elected council members is also critical to establishing continuity and implementing programs.

- **Utilities can be key partners.** The SCL Climate Wise program, with assistance from the EPA, helped build support from businesses, non-profit groups, and government agencies for energy conservation.

- **An incremental approach can be the best approach.** Seattle and King County demonstrate what can be accomplished with an incremental approach that includes beginning modestly, either with specific programs or with "piggy backing" on complementary programs, and developing measures of progress. Many of the programs that are already priorities for local governments, such as energy conservation, transportation demand management (TDM), and recycling, are programs that also reduce GHG emissions. With these programs in place, it is possible to expand this foundation of demonstrated success in order to secure commitments to support and expand climate change programs.

- **Smart growth and energy conservation are complementary policies.** Sustainability, smart growth, and energy conservation policies can be combined to support coordinated planning processes and complementary programs. These programs can then be expanded to incorporate and focus on GHG reduction goals.

- **Support from other programs can lay the groundwork for future work.** The ICLEI Climate Change Partners (CCP) program and the EPA State and Local Partners program assisted both the Seattle and King County climate change planning efforts. For example, support from the CPP program helped to lay the groundwork for Seattle's Climate Change Action Plan. The CPP program and EPA have also highlighted Seattle's experiences as examples for other areas around the country.

- **City and local efforts can complement climate change planning.** Although county and city plans may follow different institutional paths, they can still be complementary. It is important to develop working relationships with other local government agencies to address shared problems. As expressed by County Council Member Sullivan, "Air pollution [has] no borders."

- **Education and outreach can build support.** Education and outreach through regional environmental symposiums can encourage local governments to share ideas, problems, and successes.

- **Moving from supportive transit programs to linkages to transportation planning is important.** Seattle and King County transportation agencies are undertaking aggressive programs to reduce automobile use through expanded transit, ridesharing, telecommuting, demand management, and improved pedestrian and bicycle facilities. For example, Seattle projects that from 1990 to 2010, work trips taken by public transit will increase from 16 to 27 percent and work trips taken by single occupant cars will decrease from 59 to 35 percent. There may be future opportunities to demonstrate in regional or city transportation plans how these transportation strategies and reduced VMT help conserve energy, reduce GHG emissions, and meet traditional transportation goals.

6. MADISON, WISCONSIN

6.1 Introduction

On March 3, 1998, the city of Madison, Wisconsin, embarked on an environmental initiative to reduce GHG emissions by passing City Council Resolution 22941. The city, under the direction of the mayor and city council members, is working to integrate climate change and the environment into the transportation decision-making process in order to reduce GHG emissions.

Madison is a valuable example of how a local community can bring GHG issues into the transportation planning and decision-making processes. As is apparent from Table 12, Madison generates a substantial amount of GHG emissions for a city of its size.

Table 12. 1990 Comparison of GHG Emissions[35]

City	Population	Tons of CO_2	Per Capita
Ann Arbor, MI	109,600	1,694,300	15.5
Overland Park, KS	138,200	2,280,000	16.5
Schenectady, NY	149,300	1,832,700	12.3
Chula Vista, CA	168,000	1,214,000	7.2
Madison, WI	**190,800**	**3,600,600**	**18.9**
Tucson, AZ	405,400	9,527,400	23.5
Twin Cities, MN	638,700	14,000,000	21.9

[35] Source: Presentation by Jayne Somers, Environmental Engineer, Madison, WI, 2000.

6.2   Approach

In 1998, Madison Mayor Susan Bauman, Madison city council members, and local citizens began working together to help make the city a safe and healthy place to live, learn, work, and play. The group addressed many issues, including climate change. The Commission on the Environment (CoE), a board comprised of representatives from relevant city government departments, became the forum for communicating ideas on this issue. To help set the stage for and promote this effort, the mayor and city council undertook several actions and programs focused on reducing GHG.

In support of Resolution 22941, the city began to work with other communities, Dane County, and businesses in order to educate them about the impacts of climate change on Madison. On March 17, 1998, Resolution 23181 authorized the city to participate in ICLEI's CCPC. ICLEI is a voluntary international environmental agency comprised of local government members. ICLEI is working to build and serve a worldwide movement of local governments in achieving tangible improvements in global environmental and sustainable development conditions through cumulative local actions.

As part of the CCPC program, Madison developed the following goals:

- Take a leadership role in reducing GHG emissions at the local level.
- Develop a local action plan.
- Implement this effort in conjunction with other efforts to achieve environmental goals.

City staff and council members participated in a CCPC workshop and training sessions. In May 2000, the CoE approved Madison's climate protection plan. In addition, the Madison city council established a resolution to adopt the plan, including a goal of reducing GHG emissions 7 percent from 1990 baseline levels by 2010. The three most significant aspects of Madison's climate change process are the commitment of the individuals involved, the climate protection plan, and the process for implementing the plan.

6.2.1   Who Is Involved and Why

Like many other cities, Madison's initial air quality planning began to meet the ground level ozone and carbon monoxide emissions requirements set by the Clean Air Act Amendments. Since Madison is in compliance with these regulations, their current planning efforts are voluntary and in response to concerns over remaining in compliance and addressing GHG issues.

Since 1998, several key players in Madison's climate change process have emerged. Within city government, the mayor, the mayor's assistant for environmental affairs, the environmental manager, and city council members have championed climate change issues. These individuals have taken leadership roles due to concern about the environmental, public health, and economic impacts of climate change to Madison and to public support for the issue. In addition, the city's environmental manager, motor equipment superintendent, and mayor's assistant play important roles in developing, reviewing, and carrying out the goals set forth in Madison's climate protection plan.

The forums within city government in which GHG issues are discussed are the CoE and an interdepartmental staff team called the Environmental Action Team (EA Team). CoE members play an important role in working on the issues presented by the elected officials' environmental initiatives. The CoE has been a forum for environmental issues for over 20 years, demonstrating the historic importance of climate change to the Madison community. The EA Team brings together existing staff in many departments who act as champions for climate protection and who donate time towards implementing programs.

Several state and county governmental institutions have assisted Madison. Dane County is working on smart growth planning and exploring ways to implement TDM projects in Madison and it surrounding communities. Within state government, there have been two important contributors to Madison's efforts: the University of Wisconsin at Madison (UWM) and the DNR. UWM is the largest single source of GHG emissions in the city, purchasing over 9 percent of the electricity the local utility company, Madison Gas and Electric (MG&E), produces. In terms of population and infrastructure, UWM would rank as the tenth largest city in the state. The university has its own fleet of vehicles and two power plants located on its property. UWM began participating in climate change issues due to its understanding of the problem, civic responsibility, and a desire to lead by setting an example that other businesses can follow. DNR has provided guidance and grant money for climate change efforts. In addition, DNR is using its limited budget and resources to assist in implementing the state produced but not ratified Wisconsin Climate Change Action Plan.

While state and county governments and agencies are addressing climate change within the context of their own specific interests and desires, they are not explicitly linked to Madison's climate protection plan.

Within the non-governmental sector, Madison has made – and will continue to make – several partnerships with utility companies (MG&E and Alliant Energy), environmental groups, and businesses. Businesses and utility companies participate in government-sponsored environmental programs, adhere to government regulations, and provide good public relations with the community. Madison is also working with a variety of environmental groups, including SustainDane, the Wisconsin Environmental Decade, and the Madison Environmental Group. These environmental groups have participated in stakeholder meeting and helped form "eco-teams" that can address local initiatives related to GHG issues. Environmental groups participate out of civic responsibility and an interest in protecting the natural beauty of the state for environmental and recreational concerns.

6.2.2   The Climate Protection Plan

Madison's climate protection plan, a "living" document that is reviewed annually, provides the city and surrounding areas with a framework for reducing GHG emissions. The plan incorporates a five-step methodology that ICLEI helped to develop:

- Conduct an energy and emissions inventory and forecast.
- Establish an emissions target.
- Develop and obtain approval for the plan.
- Identify and implement policies that work towards the meeting the emissions target.
- Monitor, verify, and evaluate results.

The Climate Protection Plan was developed with the assistance of ICLEI through the CCPC. Resolution 22941 allowed Madison to participate in the CCPC and to receive ICLEI training and software to help develop the plan.

The main goals of Madison's climate protection plan are to create local policy measures with multiple benefits and to identify a CO_2 reduction goal. Even without an explicit CO_2 reduction goal, the plan helps the city reduce the consumption of fossil fuels and strive for a cleaner, safer, and more pedestrian friendly environment. Local actions to reduce GHG emissions provide many other benefits, including decreased air pollution, more jobs, increased energy efficiency, reduced energy expenditures, and financial savings for government agencies, businesses, and citizens.

The GHG emissions inventory for Madison was created with the help of DNR, academia, and environmental groups and consists of a detailed analysis of the sources and quantities of GHG emissions that affect the Madison area. GHG emissions in the Madison area include CO_2 and methane, which are primarily produced by the commercial sector and by utilities as they burn fossil fuels to create power. The GHG emissions inventory covers the residential, commercial, industrial, transportation, and waste sectors, as shown in Table 13.

Table 13. Break-out of Madison's 1990 CO_2 Emissions by Sector[36]

Energy Use		78%
Residential	20%	
Commercial	48%	
Industrial	10%	
Transportation		19%
Solid Waste & Landfills		3%
Note: 1 gallon of gasoline = 20 lbs of CO_2		

Energy use on commercial land is by far the biggest contributor to GHG emissions at 48 percent. Residential land use and transportation contribute nearly equally with 19 percent and 20 percent respectively.

---

[36] Source: Presentation by Jayne Somers, Environmental Engineer; Madison, WI.

The GHG emissions inventory also established forecasts for 2010. As demonstrated in Table 14, energy, transportation, and waste all are expected to grow at a rate of between 26 percent and 30 percent unless the measures in the climate protection plan are implemented.

Transportation was the second largest contributor of CO_2 in 1990 with 621,000 metric tons; this number is expected to grow to 783,000 tons by 2010. Accepting the importance of transportation to GHG emissions, the plan considers several strategies related to transportation:

- Vehicles and Roadways
- Boats and Airport Use
- Metro Transit Bus System and Rail
- Bicycles and Pedestrian Access
- Rideshare Program and Parking
- State Fleet Conversion to Alternative Fuel

Table 14. Madison GHG Emissions Inventory (Tons of CO_2)[37]

Sector	1990	2010	Growth
Energy	2,984,220	4,303,691	31%
Transportation	621,397	782,960	26%
Waste	31,489	40,936	30%
Landfills	84,863	84,863	0%
Airport	75,712	75,712	0%
Total	**3,797,681**	**5,288,162**	**29%**
Per Capita	*19.9*	*22.0*	

Many cities, along with ICLEI, recommend a GHG reduction goal of 20 percent from 1990 levels by 2010. Madison examined its resources and found this to be a difficult goal to achieve. Given the time frame, resources, and urgency the city felt, Madison selected 7 percent as a more realistic goal. While still ambitious, this was the goal for the United States under the 1997 Kyoto Protocol. To address this reduction goal, the climate protection plan identified the following program goals (Table 15):

---

[37] Source: Presentation by Jayne Somers, Environmental Engineer; Madison, WI.

Table 15. Madison: Programs and Goals

Program	Goals
Develop TDM measures	• Encourage businesses to make options like carpooling and ridesharing available to their employees. • Provide incentives to attract people to the program.
Encourage transit, rail, and bike use	• Actively market transit, rail, and bike opportunities in order to make people aware of these options. • Expand the current system as necessary and if cost effective.
Improve upon and promote fuel-efficient vehicles and their use	• Work with academia, business, and government in a regulatory capacity. • Market the cost savings of fuel-efficient vehicles.
Increase use of AFVs	• Research AFVs by funding academic research. • Encourage business and require government to invest in these vehicles for their fleets in order to lead by example.
Encourage flextime or work-at-home options	• Work with businesses and government agencies to incorporate flextime and work-at-home options into their work routine.
Continue the Sustainable Lifestyle Program	• Fund and promote environmentally friendly programs that educate people and reduce GHG emissions.
Re-examine parking policies to reduce automobile use	• Control parking to provide a disincentive for automobile use and an incentive for people who use alternate modes of travel such as walking, biking, and transit.

Madison began taking steps to implement the climate protection plan after the city council approved the plan in 2000. Outreach and education efforts began with meetings between the mayor's office, Dane County officials, and the governor's office. In addition, the city began working with several businesses and state institutions to help find ways to implement the plan's programs. For example, MG&E has had regular contact with the city to improve energy use and to expand the market for alternative vehicles by maintaining alternative fuel refueling sites. The outreach campaign is being supported with a web site and newsletter. Madison is concerned with maintaining the funding and staffing levels needed to continue implementing the plan.

6.3 Links to the Planning Process

The mayor's office and city council members identified a process agenda with the assistance of the mayor's staff and the city environmental engineer. While other partnerships may form between other participants, Madison coordinates efforts through its climate change action plan. This plan specifies what sectors of the economy contribute to GHG emissions. Complementing these efforts, the CoE identified goals and assigned objectives to individual departments within the city. In addition, the climate protection plan helped provide direction in establishing an outreach and education effort to keep stakeholders informed of how they can assist. This outreach and education effort has lead to public and private partnerships, smart growth policies, and links to local and regional transportation planning efforts. Figure 8 displays the linkages between the various governmental institutions.

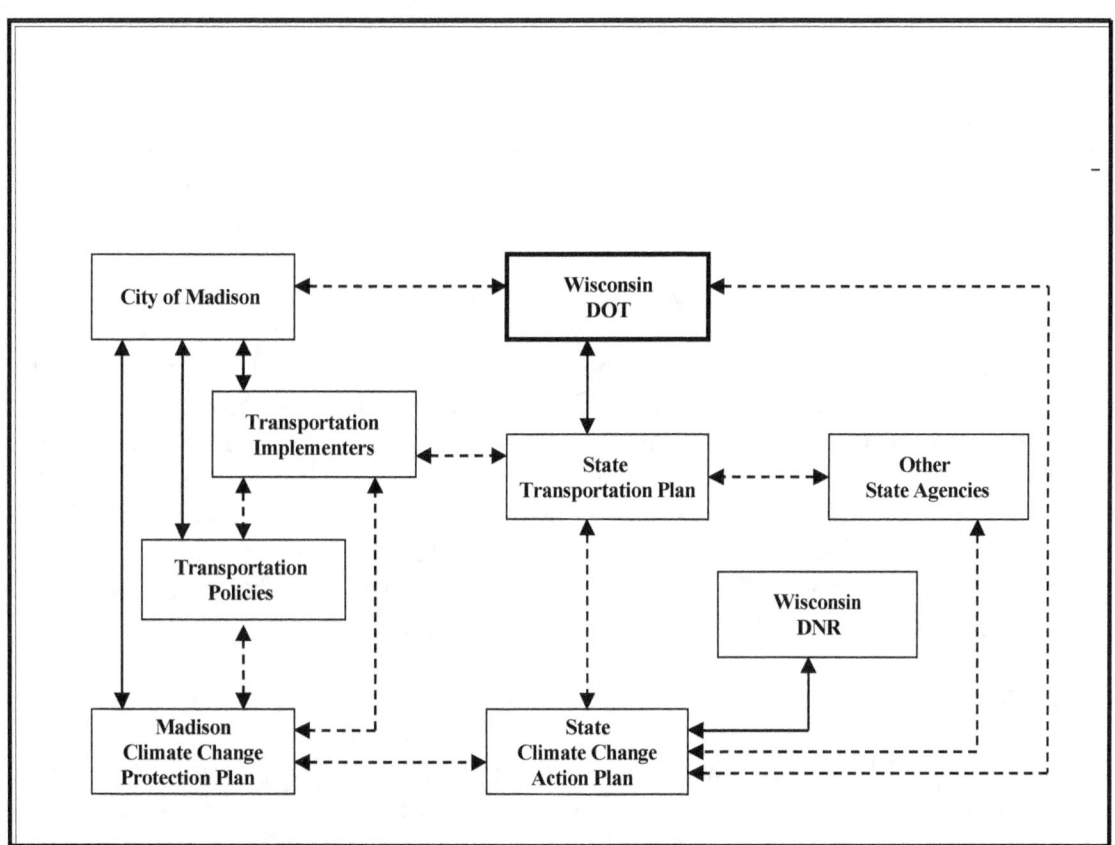

Figure 8. Climate Change and the Planning Process for GHG Draft Flow Chart of Process for City of Madison[38]

6.3.1 Energy Planning

Madison's energy policies span the residential, commercial, and industrial sectors and include government agencies, businesses, and private homes. The Madison environmental engineer

---

[38] Source: USDOT/Volpe Center, 2001.

coordinates these energy efforts using the CoE as a forum. While Madison has energy polices, it has no formal energy plan. Madison's energy policies focus on the use of Energy Star products, new energy effect buildings, green building, and expanded use of gas heating systems for the residential and commercial sectors. For the industrial sector, the policies focus on utility power plants that contribute substantial amounts of CO_2 through the burning of fossil fuels. Informal agreements with businesses, utility companies, and academia have been very important in efforts to reduce GHG emissions. As a result of Madison's outreach efforts, MG&E and Alliant Energy are converting voluntarily to gas-fired plants when opportunities arise and expanding their existing wind power systems by 2005. In addition, the UWM's two steam generation plants will use more alternative fuels in the future.

6.3.2   Transportation Planning

The effort to reduce GHG emissions through the transportation planning process is led by Madison but also includes Dane County, the MPO, and the state DOT in advisory and supportive roles. The city is taking the lead on several issues like transit, TDM, and parking, including these strategies in their planning process. While not explicitly linked, the climate protection plan identifies issues that the city should address. Some options focus on Executive Orders from the mayor's office to identify the vision, such as making the city fleet a "green fleet" of AFVs.

Dane County and the MPO are working cooperatively with Madison to increase the use of AFVs and sustainable growth policies that consider establishing eco-teams and regulating land use. The MPO's long-range transportation plan and the Madison transportation plan are directly linked. While the state and EPA contribute funding to help move these projects forward, they do not have links to Madison's transportation planning process since Madison is in attainment for air quality and SIP requirements. Though the city government generally controls Madison's transportation planning process, it has involved businesses in the planning process. The city has built a partnership with utility companies to provide refueling stations that can be used by the city, county, and state's growing fleets of AFVs. The city is also working with businesses to increase the use of ridesharing and carpools by their employees.

6.4   Results to Date

By comparing the goals defined in the climate protection plan and early indications, it is evident that Madison has had some initial success in addressing climate change issues. First, Madison developed and garnered acceptance of the climate protection plan. Without the support of a majority of the people involved and the acceptance of the city council, the initiative would have probably failed. Second, according to local sources, Madison reduced CO_2 emissions by over 100,000 tons per year. Third, Madison's outreach efforts fostered cooperation between different departments; now, these departments can work together to determine what is and is not working to improve energy efficiency. The Madison Planning Department and area utilities are working to improve energy efficiency, but their work is still in its early stages.

66

Transportation has been addressed at various levels, including state input to the transportation planning process and local government partnerships with businesses to promote ridesharing. Madison's Green Fleet program to replace some of their current vehicles with hybrid electric vehicles is underway, but it is a long-term, costly project. The UWM and the State of Wisconsin DOA are also working to make their vehicle fleets more "green." The Madison U.S. Postal Service's fleet is considering installing ethanol fueling facilities through a state grant. Madison has partnered with energy companies to invest in the CNG, ethanol, and biodiesel infrastructure and refueling sites needed to support the Green Fleet program. In addition, the city is currently attempting to form a clean cities coalition of local fleet managers who will pledge to use ethanol and biodiesel fuels so that fueling facilities can be built.

The biggest unknown is establishing financial sources to support these projects. Madison has made an effort to incorporate some items, like vehicle purchases, directly into their budget and dedicate staff and time to support these issues. To date, the city has had limited success in receiving grant money for these programs. Grant money will be even more difficult to get in the future due to poor economic conditions. Although funding for environmental initiatives has remained fairly constant over the last several years, more and more cities have become involved in ICLEI's CCPC program. In the last three years, the number of city memberships has nearly doubled. As a result, more cities are competing for a fixed amount of money.

6.5 How the Process Has Evolved

In response to the climate change action plan's commitment to annual updates, Madison is currently going through its first annual assessment to determine the success of its climate protection plan. The city will identify where improvements are needed, and updates will continue through 2010. The success of Madison's climate change efforts will depend on the availability of funds for projects and programs, continued political support, and project cost effectiveness. Where possible, Madison will expand programs currently underway, including the Green Fleet program, TDM measures, the newsletter, and partnerships with businesses. Though expensive, Madison has included the purchase of hybrid electric, CNG, and other AFVs included in its budget. As the mayor of Madison appoints department heads, approves the budget, and helps shape the city's agenda, any change in leadership in the mayor's office or in city departments could change priorities. However, the main climate change forum, supported by the CoE and local environmental groups, will remain relatively constant.

6.6 Lessons Learned

Madison provides a valuable example of how a city can take a leadership role on climate change issues. Several factors have fostered Madison's ability to formulate a plan, gain support for recommendations, and implement actions:

- **Political champions play a key role.** Support and cooperation from the mayor's office, city council members, and the public were critical to the success of Madison's climate protection plan.

- **Long-term environmental commitment is invaluable.** The Madison climate change plan was supported by the community's tradition of placing a high value on the environment, as can be seen by the creation of the CoE. In setting their agenda, elected officials have emphasized the environment and, most recently, the issue of climate change.

- **Linking climate change and energy policies can promote energy efficiency.** Madison's efforts demonstrate how a climate change plan can be closely linked to energy planning to improve energy efficiency.

- **Peer comparisons play a critical role.** Developers of the climate protection plan effectively used performance measures and benchmarks, such as GHG emissions per capita of peer cities and sectoral contributions to the city baseline, to gain interest and support.

- **Developing a climate change plan can promote future action.** The creation and endorsement of the climate protection plan by the city enabled participants in the planning process to focus on climate change issues and to address them by sector.

- **Outside support can provide a valuable foundation.** The Madison climate protection plan was created with the aid of the ICLEI and was directed by dedicated staff appointed by the mayor's office. ICLEI provided training for elected officials and staff and a suggested framework that included determining baseline GHG emissions and sources, setting reductions goals, and developing an action plan.

- **Setting realistic goals promotes success.** The reduction goals the city set for itself were based on conservative and realistic estimates of what the city thought it could achieve in a 10-year time frame. The city also supplemented its reduction goals with annual reviews against benchmarks that it established.

- **Taking a practical approach supports actions.** The programs Madison created to address climate change goals were selected based on political support and demonstrated cost effectiveness. The programs were financed by grants, matching federal funds, and partnerships with businesses.

III. OBSERVATIONS AND CONCLUSION

States and local areas are making impressive and surprising progress in developing plans to reduce GHG emissions. Twenty-five states have GHG action plans, and 134 cities and counties participate in a GHG planning program that includes commitments to pass supportive resolutions, conduct baseline estimates, develop action plans, and monitor results. States and local areas are undertaking these initiatives voluntarily: there are no federal requirements for GHG emission reduction such as those of the Clean Air Act Amendments for air quality conformity. These efforts are largely ad hoc, although there are increasing exchanges of information on state and local initiatives supported through programs of the EPA, ICLEI, the Pew Center, or the Center for Clean Air Policy. Also, there are very modest resources available through EPA and ICLEI to encourage state and local GHG planning.

The following observations are derived from the states and local areas studied.

- **A coordinated formal approach is important**. The planning elements used in the case study areas provide a framework for interested states and local areas to adapt to their unique situations. The plans developed in the case study areas have most, if not all, of the following elements:
  - Description of regional impacts.
  - Quantitative assessment of baseline GHG emissions, usually by sector, through forecast models and data analysis.
  - GHG emissions reduction goals or a range of targets for analysis.
  - Scenarios to assess trade-offs among sectors and strategies to meet the goals set.
  - Attempts to provide measures of cost-effectiveness to evaluate alternative strategies.
  - Action plan with recommended strategies.
  - Provisions to evaluate results and adjust accordingly.

  This framework provides a useful alternative to taking an ad hoc approach to beginning a new GHG plan. It can also be supplemented by using information, training, and technical tools provided by the ICLEI and the EPA State and Local Partners program. There are important opportunities to expand these types of resources to include a transportation planning focus.

- **Climate change impacts can be used as points of departure**. Recognition of the regional impacts states or local areas face from climate change can be a critical impetus for developing GHG plans. Impacts reflect the unique vulnerabilities of each area – shorelines in New Jersey, Oregon, and Washington, for example, or forests and tourism in New Hampshire. Shared concern about regional impacts can provide a key impetus even when participants accept that causes of regional impacts are global and that local reductions will not produce measurable changes.

69

- **Motivation to act does not come solely from concern over impacts**. State and local areas may conduct GHG planning out of a sense of local responsibility and a need to contribute to actions underway in other areas, but areas may also participate in GHG planning out of a pragmatic understanding that climate change goals can strengthen other state and local initiatives. These initiatives can include energy conservation to reduce costs and vulnerability and growth management.

- **Smart growth and energy conservation planning can provide the foundation for climate change planning**. Climate change planning does not appear to originate in isolation of other related concerns and with independent political champions and constituencies. Typically, it follows the development of policies and plans in related policy areas, such as smart growth and energy conservation. The perception appears to be that public and political support for climate change, energy, or smart growth goals can be complementary and mutually supportive. In fact, planning to reduce GHG emissions often has its foundation in state or local policies for energy (i.e., conservation and development of alternative sources and industries), and smart growth (i.e., land use and economic development considerations).

- **Political champions play a critical role**. Political champions play a critical role in initiating GHG plans. In all seven case studies, GHG plans moved forward because of the leadership of governors, mayors, and legislative leaders. The involvement of such political champions makes it more likely that participation in GHG planning will extend beyond energy or environmental sectors to include the transportation sector as it, too, is under executive authority. However, reliance on political champions can place the long-term commitment needed for GHG planning and implementation at risk because the administrations can shift.

- **Non-transportation agencies are playing lead roles**. Much of the impetus for state and local GHG plans appears to come from state and local agencies with primary responsibility for non-transportation sectors such as energy, environment, and land use. GHG plans developed under the lead of these non-transportation agencies universally tend to recognize the major contribution of transportation to GHG emissions baselines and the importance of including transportation actions in GHG emissions reduction planning and programs. State and local transportation planning and operating agencies typically participate, but do not play lead roles, in the early stages of GHG planning. There may be important opportunities for these agencies to play more active roles in this important aspect of transportation and environmental planning.

- **The transportation sector appears to lag behind in GHG emissions reduction planning.** Although the transportation sector is consistently identified as a major source of GHG emissions, transportation policies, strategies, and actions to reduce emissions typically lag behind those for other sectors. In contrast to the proposed actions to reduce GHG emissions for other sectors, the transportation actions recommended tend to be more conceptual, framed as general policy, and less specific in terms of timetables and institutional responsibilities for implementation.

It would be worthwhile to assess in greater depth why links to the transportation sector are so difficult to form and how this might be overcome. This is an area where additional "best practices" case studies and funding for pilot projects to experiment with and objectively evaluate innovative technical and institutional approaches might be productive.

- **A range of institutional approaches and integration methods exists.** No single best approach exists for defining institutional roles and responsibilities to successfully integrate climate change and transportation planning. The seven case study areas include models for city, county, state, and multi-state/bi-national initiatives. In some cases, city or county and state plans are mutually supportive; in other cases, they proceed independently. If these GHG planning initiatives continue to be robust and evolve, they will find other opportunities to strengthen links between plans and strategies in these dimensions:
  - **Vertically** – to connect state, regional, and city and county GHG planning.
  - **Horizontally** – to connect transportation, GHG, environmental, and land use planning done by a state, region, city, or county.

- **Success depends on a broad base of support and long-term commitment**. The case study areas demonstrate that moving from the ideals of a GHG plan to the actual implementation of plan actions is difficult and requires a long-term time horizon and the cooperation of different levels of government, different economic sectors, and public and private partners. Clearly, a broad base of political and public support is essential for success. Delaware demonstrated this fact with its broad base of institutional and personal commitment to a long-term planning process.

- **Incremental progress is valuable**. Several case study areas recognized the value of demonstrating early incremental progress, including beginning with strategies where benefits clearly surpass financial and political costs and where lead agencies have direct responsibility. Case study areas describe incremental progress as finding "win-win" strategies or as identifying the "low hanging fruit." For example, some areas began by partnering with utilities and their customers, demonstrating that energy savings and reduced GHG emissions can be accomplished with modest public investments. Early progress demonstrates how the planning process can proceed successfully, establishes the technical and institutional credibility of the planning process, and provides participants with positive, demonstrative results. Early progress also helps overcome the reluctance of future participants to risk traditional goals and projects by participating in the GHG planning process.

- **It is difficult to tell if the glass is "half empty" or "half full."** The extent of linkages between transportation planning and GHG planning is a matter of perspective. It is difficult to tell if the glass is "half empty" or "half full." Explicit linkages to transportation planning are at an early stage, newly formed, and rapidly evolving. The case study areas presented uniformly recognize the significant contribution that the transportation sector makes to baseline GHG emissions and the important role that transportation may play in meeting voluntary targets. Typically, these case study areas consider it difficult to include GHG goals in the transportation planning process, but worth pursuing.

- **Continued evolution will be necessary to move from indirect supportive actions to explicit planning**. The case study areas already pursue strategies for smart growth/livability, congestion, and air quality improvements that also reduce GHG emissions. Portland, Seattle, and Madison have direct operational responsibilities for major transportation programs, making it easier for them to implement transportation actions in their GHG plans. Seattle transportation agencies are implementing aggressive programs to reduce automobile use through expanded transit, ridesharing, telecommuting, and improved pedestrian and bicycle facilities.

  There are opportunities to further develop climate change plans by building on these areas' supportive programs. Expanding and improving these programs could provide future opportunities for state DOTs, MPOs, city transportation agencies, and transportation operators (e.g., public transit, rail, air, or maritime) interested in integrating climate change goals into transportation planning processes. As a result, explicit consideration should be given to how these transportation strategies and reduced VMT contribute to conserving energy, reducing GHG emissions, and meeting traditional transportation goals.

- **Opportunities exist to expand linkages.** There are important opportunities for states and local areas to strengthen climate change planning by expanding linkages to transportation planning. The case study areas are making efforts to expand linkages between planning for GHG reductions and transportation planning by state DOTs, MPOs, local areas, and transportation operators. For example, New Jersey will emphasize the transportation sector following the state's earlier emphases on industry, utilities, and education.

  The future challenge for the case study and other areas will be to elevate political and public awareness of climate change concerns to allow MPOs, regional transportation authorities, or state DOTs to consider GHG reduction goals explicitly alongside traditional transportation goals in planning future policies and investments.

- **Peer experiences can demonstrate successful GHG planning**. States and local areas are very interested in descriptions and documentation of successful GHG planning by peers. Such peer exchanges may be the best way to demonstrate that climate change goals and planning can be introduced in a rational manner without threatening the goals and programs of transportation agencies. One case study area contact noted, "Our commissioner is much more interested in the positive first-hand experiences of his peers than in technical reports and analyses. He needs to know that it can be done and how and would value hearing this from a peer." Clearly, a great opportunity exists to encourage state and local planning through peer exchanges, objective evaluations, and "best practice" examples.

- **Additional research would prove valuable**. This study provides a perspective on how several states and local areas are beginning to integrate GHG emission reduction goals into transportation planning. Each area adapts its process technically and institutionally to meet difficult challenges. It would be worthwhile to track this evolution, including lessons learned and actual GHG emission reductions. Additional research would prove worthwhile, as this study is not intended to critically examine the assumptions, methods, data, or likely success of each case study area's initiatives to reduce GHG emissions. Such a critical examination is beyond the scope of this limited study. It would be extremely valuable for the USDOT CCCEF or another independent entity to undertake such an objective assessment in the future.

Appendix A. States with Greenhouse Gas Plans

According to the EPA, as of May 2001, 25 states and Puerto Rico had initiated state action plans and 19 states had completed action plans. On the map below (Figure A1), those states with completed action plans are darkly shaded. Those with plans in progress are shaded lightly.[39]

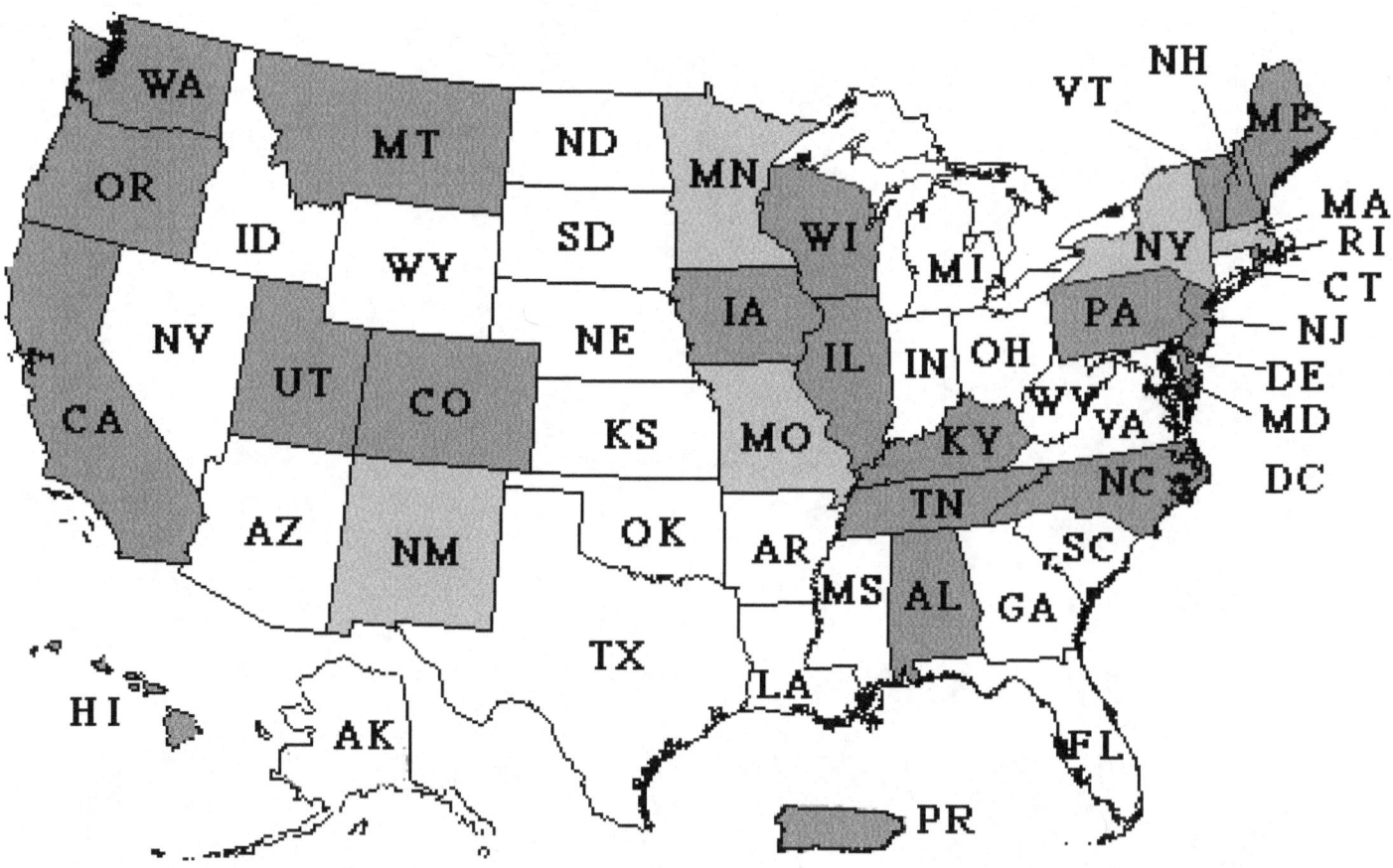

Figure A1. States with GHG Plans

---

[39] Source: http://yosemite.epa.gov/globalwarming/ghg.nsf/actions/StateActionPlans?Open#Plans.

Appendix B. Cities and Counties in ICLEI's Cities for Climate Protection Program

Ann Arbor and Washtenaw County, MI

Arlington County, VA

Aspen, CA

Atlanta, GA

Austin, TX

Berkeley, CA

Brattleboro, VT

Burlington, VT

Cambridge, MA

Carrboro, NC

Chapel Hill, NC

Chattanooga, TN

Chicago, IL

Chula Vista, CA

Decatur, GA

Denver, CO

Duluth, MN

Honolulu, HI

Irvine, CA

Los Angeles, CA

Louisville, KY

Louisville and Jefferson County, KY

Madison, WI

Miami Dade County, FL

Minneapolis, MN

Muncie, IN

Newark, NJ

New York, NY

Olympia, WA

Overland Park, KS

Portland, OR

San Diego, CA

San Francisco, CA

Santa Cruz, CA

Santa Monica, CA

Santa Rosa, CA

Seattle, WA

Sebastopol, CA

Tacoma Park, WA

Tucson, AZ

Appendix C. List of Acronyms

AFV	Alternative Fuel Vehicle
AQST	Air Quality Steering Team
CAFE	Corporate Average Fuel Economy
CCCEF	Center for Climate Change and Environmental Forecasting
CCP	Climate Change Partners
CCPC	Cities for Climate Protection Campaign
CNG	Compressed Natural Gas
CoE	Commission on the Environment
DelDOT	Delaware Department of Transportation
DNR	Department of Natural Resources
DOE	Department of Energy
EA Team	Environmental Action Team
EARA	Environmental Auditors Registration Association
EIA	Energy Information Agency
EPA	Environmental Protection Agency
EPAct	Energy Policy Act
GHG	Greenhouse Gas
ICLEI	International Council for Local Environmental Initiatives
ISTEA	Intermodal Surface Transportation Efficiency Act
LAP	Local Action Plan on Global Warming
MG&E	Madison Gas & Electric
MPO	Metropolitan Planning Organization
NEG-ECP	New England Governors and Eastern Canadian Premiers
NEGC	New England Governors' Conference
NEPPS	National Environmental Performance Partnership System
NICE	Northeast International Committee on Energy
NJDEP	New Jersey Department of Environmental Protection
NJDOT	New Jersey Department of Transportation
NPP	Neighborhood Power Project
NRTEE	National Round Table on the Environment and the Economy
OOE	Oregon Office of Energy
RTP	Regional Transportation Plan
SCL	Seattle City Light

SEO	State Energy Office
SGGAP	Sustainability Greenhouse Gas Action Plan
TCM	Transportation Control Measures
TDM	Transportation Demand Management
TEA-21	Transportation Equity Act for the 21st Century
TSP	Transportation System Plan
USDOT	U.S. Department of Transportation
UWM	University of Wisconsin at Madison
VMT	Vehicle Miles Traveled
Volpe Center	Volpe National Transportation Systems Center

www.ingramcontent.com/pod-product-compliance
Lightning Source LLC
Chambersburg PA
CBHW052005280526
45793CB00005B/854

* 9 7 8 1 4 9 9 3 3 4 2 3 4 *